ACTS OF FICTION

PENN STATE STUDIES
in ROMANCE LITERATURES

Editors
Frederick A. de Armas
Alan E. Knight

Refiguring the Hero:
From Peasant to Noble in Lope de Vega and Calderón
by Dian Fox

Don Juan and the Point of Honor:
Seduction, Patriarchal Society, and Literary Tradition
by James Mandrell

Narratives of Desire:
Nineteenth-Century Spanish Fiction by Women
by Lou Charnon-Deutsch

Garcilaso de la Vega and the Italian Renaissance
by Daniel L. Heiple

Allegories of Kingship:
Calderón and the Anti-Machiavellian Tradition
by Stephen Rupp

Acts of Fiction:
Resistance and Resolution from Sade to Baudelaire
by Scott Carpenter

Scott Carpenter

●

ACTS OF FICTION

Resistance and Resolution from Sade to Baudelaire

The Pennsylvania State University Press
University Park, Pennsylvania

Library of Congress Cataloging-in-Publication Data

Carpenter, Scott, 1958–
    Acts of fiction : resistance and resolution from Sade to
Baudelaire / Scott Carpenter.
            p.   cm.
    Includes bibliographical references and index.
    ISBN 0-271-01450-4 (cloth)
    ISBN 0-271-01449-0 (paper)
    1. French literature—19th century—History and criticism.
2. Sade, marquis de, 1740–1814—Criticism and interpretation.
3. Balzac, Honoré de, 1799–1850—Criticism and interpretation.
4. Nerval, Gérard de, 1808–1855—Criticism and interpretation.
5. Baudelaire, Charles, 1821–1867—Criticism and interpretation.
6. Modernism (Literature)—France.   7. Narration (Rhetoric)
I. Title.
PQ288.C37   1996
840.9′007—dc20   94-42527
                                                                    CIP

Published by The Pennsylvania State University Press,
University Park, PA 16802-1003

It is the policy of The Pennsylvania State University Press to use acid-free paper for
the first printing of all clothbound books. Publications on uncoated stock satisfy the
minimum requirements of American National Standard for Information Sciences—
Permanence of Paper for Printed Library Materials, ANSI Z39.48–1992.

To Anne

"Dieu nous préserve des lectures inutiles."
—Baudelaire, citing Lavater

Contents

List of Illustrations

Acknowledgments

Without a leave funded by the American Council of Learned Societies and the National Endowment for the Humanities, this book would surely still rest in a pile of poorly organized manila folders, buried under exams, papers, and theses; I cannot adequately express my gratitude to these institutions. In addition, I am extremely grateful to Carleton College for its generous support, both financial and temporal.

The most crucial help, however, comes not from institutions, but from individuals. I extend special thanks to Alan Astro, Frank Bowman, John Greene, Michele Hannoosh, John Martin, Adrianna Paliyenko, Lauren Pinzka, Peter Schofer, Dana Strand, Matt Stroud, Michael Weissenstein, and Cathy Yandell. Also of great assistance was the staff of the Bibliothèque Nationale in Paris, both in the Département des Imprimés and in the Cabinet des Estampes. Finally, my wife, Anne Maple, served as an indispensable audience, critic, and supporter, especially in the early stages of the work.

Part of Chapter 2 first appeared in *Neophilologus,* vol. 75 (1991), and a portion of Chapter 4 appeared in *Nineteenth-Century French Studies,* vol. 17 (Fall–Winter 1988–89); the editors of these journals have kindly allowed me to reprint the passages in question.

A Note on Translations

All French passages are quoted in English translation; in the case of poetry, or passages of special subtlety, the original has also been included. Unless otherwise indicated, translations are my own.

Introduction

During the Soviet invasion of Czechoslovakia in the spring of 1968, the Prague citizenry came up with an unusual form of resistance. In a subtle and pacific act of sabotage, they began removing, relocating, and repainting street signs all across the city, thereby transforming the capital into a Borgesian labyrinth and seriously disorienting the occupying troops. In the weeks that followed there ensued a peculiar struggle: with the Czechs rewriting their city under the cover of night and the Soviets attempting to decipher it during the day, the two sides fought a battle over signs.[1]

There is something particularly modern about this state of affairs. For one thing, it is played out in a semiotic field, where the endless substitution of signs for other signs is irreducibly metaphoric. Here political authority is determined by the most successful rhetorical gambit, the one that makes its signs "stick." The episode illustrates how power is linked to, or even defined by, control over the symbolic.[2] While the stability of signs helps to fix meanings and to qualify them as usual or even natural for their users, the Prague episode points to the fragility of signifying systems. It reminds us of their arbitrariness and shows how disorienting changes in them can be.

Authority lobbies against such disruptions, and when powers come into conflict, when several voices strive to stake their claim on the same signs, we are made to feel as if we are living in Prague. Indeed, given the modern dissatisfaction with the ability of words to anchor meaning, and the general suspicion that something is fiddling with our signs, one might surmise that we have all been "living in Prague" for quite some

1. See Christian Brunier ("Tchécoslovaquie 1968," 82). My thanks to Jim Long for drawing my attention to this episode of modern history.
2. This can also be seen in another form of popular resistance during the Prague Spring. As local radio stations went underground, transmitting from a variety of locations, the authorities were confronted with other questions typical of the modern quandry: Who is speaking? And from where?

time. Signs have simply become unreliable, their relationship to the things they depict being tenuous at best. As a result of struggles such as that between the Soviet invaders and the Czech resistance, signs have gone adrift from fixed meanings; indeed, they show an unsettling *resistance* to meaning, a resistance it has proved impossible to check.

This problem with words and other signs may be modern, but it is certainly nothing new. Seemingly transparent language—which will here be associated with the classical imagination—enjoyed its last hurrah in the middle of the eighteenth century. In domains especially sensitive to issues of representation, the end of the Enlightenment marked the beginning of a new and disturbing age, and words would never act the same again. Yet reactions to this shift, while immediate, were not uniform, and this is something that critical retrospectives have glossed over. Recent narrators of the transition (working in the wake of Michel Foucault, Roland Barthes, Julia Kristeva) have presented the modern sensibility as something like a phoenix rising fully formed from the ashes of the classical age. In an effort to focus on that which is definitively modern, they have directed their gaze upon figures of the late nineteenth century (Mallarmé, Laurtéamont, Nietzsche) for whom the disintegration of the reliable sign is a fait accompli.

Yet in order to appreciate the struggle from which the modern sensibility was to emerge, one must look earlier. What the gaze upon the modern has overlooked is the movement between periods, the shifting from the classical to the modern, the period of transition. The example of the Prague Spring suggests that battles over signs become especially urgent at times of revolution (political or otherwise). When there are sweeping redefinitions of the cultural world, symbolic constructions serve to impose order on new chaos, renegotiating the relationship between individuals and social reality. The cultural shift that began around the time of the French Revolution is one such moment. Yet the transition was not abrupt; for all its explosiveness, the Revolution did not spend itself in a sudden discharge of energy. Launching France on a political roller-coaster ride during which it careened through eleven constitutions in rather fewer decades, pitching back and forth between democracy and despotism, the Revolution may be said to have extended through the end of the Second Empire. Moreover, the upheaval was as cultural as it was political, and acts of resistance translated into acts of fiction as attempts were made to put a mercurial present—and one that was increasingly suspicious of symbolic solutions—into some definition.

The present volume undertakes to investigate literary reactions to this cultural shift. It focuses on an expanded revolutionary period, ranging from the disintegration of classical models in the second half of the eighteenth century to what might be thought of as the institutionalization of the modern after the middle of the nineteenth. In this space, which both separates and joins two ages, are located works of capital importance: those of Laclos, Sade, Balzac, Nerval, and Baudelaire, among others. These are authors of transition who, confronted with a foundering classical imagination, are unsure how to respond. Nevertheless, in their writings these transitional figures reveal the modes of reaction available to them, as well as the rhetorical gambits they developed for coming to terms with a nascent modernity. Their strategies are invariably plays for power; as such they highlight the articulation between language and authority, between narrative and meaning.

1 Traveling *Mis*cognito: Revolution and Symbolic Resolution

Let us begin with an ending.

The conclusion of Laclos's libertine novel, *Dangerous Liaisons* (1782), is marked by a terrific reversal of fortune: Valmont and the Présidente de Tourvel die, Cécile retreats to a convent while Danceny sets sail for Malta, and the commanding marquise de Merteuil—the arch-libertine—falls victim to the double afflictions of smallpox and public opinion. It is Madame de Volanges, the long-duped and prudish mother of Cécile, who, in one of her rare letters, has the last word. Relating the details of the marquise's fate, she notes,

> I was right to say that she might have been better off dying of her pox. It is true that she recovered, but horribly disfigured; in particular, she has lost an eye.... The marquis de ***, who never foregoes an opportunity to slight someone, said of her yesterday that the illness had turned her inside out, and that she now wears her soul on her face. Unfortunately, everyone found the expression quite apt. (Laclos, 378)

Repelled by society, the marquise de Merteuil vanishes in a self-imposed exile, absconding with what remains of her family fortune.

What is one to make of Laclos's precipitous, moralizing conclusion? One can read in the final letter either a hack attempt to pass the novel off as a lesson in virtue or, alternatively, as an ironic spoof of such moralizations; both readings are common.[1] Either way, however, one thing is clear: no matter how we interpret this passage, the final letter allows for closure. In quite pedestrian terms, we might say that the novel has staged a problem (call it "libertinism"), a problem that when "resolved" (Valmont and Merteuil die or disappear), leaves us with nowhere to go; so, the novel comes to a halt.

It should come as no surprise that the novel's ending coincides with its resolution: conclusion and resolution are part of the essence of narrative and other forms of symbolic behavior.[2] In at least a formal sense, closure functions as a defining characteristic of symbolic constructions: plots run their course, musical themes exhaust their possibilities, paint reaches the edge of its canvas. Even individual sentences aim for a completeness that we recognize by punctuation. It should be just as obvious that this formal closure is precisely what eludes the nonfictional or nonsymbolic: events (though they may be interpreted otherwise) know no tidy boundaries; matter itself extends, messily, forever. Thus attempts (even the most avant-garde) to reproduce events or experiences symbolically must always be inadequate: closure functions as an artificial containment of that which is potentially interminable.[3] Symbolic behavior has thus been described as an artifice that allows us to manage, handle, and manipulate that which "in reality" escapes our control.[4] In *Dangerous Liaisons*, for example, one might speculate that the novel

---

1. For a survey of some of these interpretations, see Byrne, "The Moral of *Les Liaisons dangereuses*." On the irreducible ambiguity of the ending, see Joan DeJean, *Literary Fortifications*, 6.

2. See especially Lévi-Strauss, *Pensée sauvage,* 26–33; and, more recently, Fredric Jameson, *Political Unconscious,* and Ross Chambers, *Room for Maneuver*. Richard Rorty has gone so far as to elevate fiction (and the uses to which it is put) to the pinnacle of pragmatist philosophy. See his response to Umberto Eco in Eco's *Interpretation and Overinterpretation,* 89–108.

3. See Torgovnick, 3–4. Closure is illusory even in forms of art that seek to bridge the gap between reality and artifice, as in Marcel Duchamp's clever ready-mades, or certain modern musical pieces that rely on accidental background noise. Still, even these works are "framed" (thus artificially enclosed) in time or space.

4. Jameson refers to this as narrative's ability to propose an "imaginary resolution" (*Political Unconscious,* 77). In the Lacanian model, the Symbolic order functions as a means of compensating for the Real.

reproduces a "problem" that was meaningful for its readership (say, the perception of corruption among the aristocracy of the late eighteenth century), and that it "resolves" this problem (by the apparent restoration of morality) in a way readers could not hope to realize in the broader field of society.

This view of fiction as "symbolic resolution" is one that has gained considerable currency in theoretical schools as diverse as Lacanian psychoanalysis and Marxism. But the notion does not mean that narratives turn into mere wish fulfillment, either personal or social; rarely does "anything go." We might very much wish, for example, that we could believe in the divine right of monarchs (say, Louis XVI, reigning at the time *Dangerous Liaisons* appeared), but narratives or other symbolic representations (such as coronations) that tell us it is so make as little headway with a modern audience as stories asserting that Santa Claus exists. Telling a story does not necessarily satisfy our desire. Stories involving Santa Claus or divine right generally breach certain terms (*vraisemblance*, for example) that the modern reader may require in a narrative contract: we may see an avuncular Saint Nick—or Louis XVI for that matter—as too blatant a stand-in for unconditional, parental love. A child, however, more broad-minded about what she or he reads, less finicky about some of the details that trouble us, and perhaps more desperate for the experience, may discover the satisfaction we would have liked to be able to find, thereby enjoying the resolutions offered by the fiction. Adults cannot enjoy the story of Santa Claus in the same way children do (though they may enjoy it in other ways) precisely because they understand how at least one aspect of it works: they recognize it as a magical narrative. As for Father Christmas, so for the father figures of states: as soon as we understand that the divine right of monarchs is a symbolic ruse to grant legitimacy, the symbol fails to persuade us of that legitimacy. It would appear that successful fictions require their public to overlook the fact that their resolutions are "merely" symbolic: narrative efficacy requires readerly misrecognition. Generally speaking, when fiction shows its hand, revealing that it is a solution *only* symbolically, that its closure is *only* artificial, it ceases to be effective. When, like Dorothy in the land of Oz, we see "the man behind the curtain," much of the wizardry is lost.

This general principle appears to hold for most forms of symbolic behavior. René Girard, for example, has shown that the public's ignorance of the symbolic nature of ritual is essential to its appreciation of sacrificial rites. "As we have seen," he writes, "the sacrificial process requires a certain degree of *misunderstanding*. The celebrants do not and *must not* comprehend the true role of the sacrificial act."[5] In fact, this "rule of ignorance" can be generalized: political discourse, when it becomes so heavy-handed that one can read it only as propaganda, no longer works its subtle magic; in psychoanalysis nothing impedes the transference more than a patient's awareness of the mechanics of transference; if, as Marx suggested, religion is the opiate of the masses, it becomes distinctly less intoxicating for those who suddenly see it as such. Even in such "lifeless" fictions as scholarly writing illusions abound. When composing drafts of an academic piece (this chapter for example), we propose rhetorical solutions for theoretical problems. One may circumvent the impossible task of presenting hopelessly complex material by limiting oneself to a synedochic sample, where one hopes the part will represent the whole;[6] or, in order to distill ideas for others, one may resort to rapid, imperfect analogies. When we write ourselves into one corner, we rewrite ourselves into another, more comfortable one, occasionally creating little more than an illusion of logic by the artful repetition of the phrases and constructions that denote rigorous argumentation.

But writing has always meant making the best of a bad situation. Indeed, one of the most prominent theoretical movements of the last decade did nothing if not show that logical impasses are endemic to writing, even among writers who seek most avidly to navigate around them.[7] Only when the inevitable sleight-of-hand escapes notice can the presentation work. Symbolic solutions need to travel "*mis*cognito," not just unnoticed, but actually mistaken for something else.

At issue, ultimately, is narrative power, that uncanny ability of fiction to make us suspend our disbelief and, as often as not, our analysis. Narrative success depends on this manipulation of its audience, for when we learn the mechanics of a symbolic construction, we subtract ourselves from its control; although we may admire the apparatus, we cease

---

5. *Violence and the Sacred,* 7; emphasis added. In a recent study, Lynn Hunt has brought Girard's analyses to bear on the period of the French Revolution (*Family Romance,* 53–88).

6. The resultant distortion leads us to speak, necessarily, of such fictional constructs as "the classical imagination," as if an age were univocal and monolithic. For better or worse, the term will recur in this chapter with some frequency.

7. See especially Paul de Man, *Blindness and Insight.*

to be susceptible to it in the same way.[8] In short, analysis empowers the reader, but it does so *at the expense of the text*. This is why the most compelling works—that is, those that continue to enthrall us (in every sense of the word)—are those that best resist the critical onslaught, never revealing the entirety of their symbolic functioning.

This book deals with the way in which fictions consolidate their power. In particular, it focuses on a period when the adequacy and legitimacy of symbolic resolutions as a whole had come radically into question, beginning in the late eighteenth century. It is at this time that the classical imagination—which I shall characterize by a faith in the transparency of signs and symbols—began to disintegrate.

Of Libertines and Language

The symptoms of this disintegration are already inscribed within *Dangerous Liaisons*, where symbolic disintegration is linked to the failing integrity of other important constructions. Laclos's novel taps into popular discontent with the perceived decadence of the aristocracy, but it reaches well beyond the merely "local" context of Parisian high society.[9] Subtending and fueling Laclos's plot was the eighteenth-century fascination with the cultural Other (Douthwaite, 4–15). In works ranging from Montesquieu's *Lettres persanes* (1721) to Graffigny's *Lettres d'une péruvienne* (1747), to Bougainville's *Voyage autour du monde* (1771) and to Diderot's *Supplément au voyage de Bougainville* (1772), the hunt for the Other led in uncomfortable directions, with "otherness" never quite appearing where it was thought to reside. Thus, in the *Lettres persanes* the exotic difference Usbek seeks does not lie among the French (nor does Usbek, who is Persian in dress alone, become exotic for the French reader). Rather, what remains irremediably foreign to Usbek is the home he has left and, more specifically, Roxane, the one wife whom he had mistakenly believed to have understood.[10] In *Lettres*

---

8. And it is precisely a nostalgia for "naive" reading that has led recently to an appeal by some for so-called ecstatic, noninterpretative reading.

9. This perception will be dealt with further in Chapter 2.

10. Indeed, the exotic difference of the Persian travelers is so superficial that Rica complains of a loss of attention when he trades his Persian costume for more Western garments (Montesquieu, 66).

d'une péruvienne, the foreign protagonist, Zilia, displays considerable independence and sufficient mastery over the narrative so as to establish *herself* as the cultural center; meanwhile, her French hosts come off as the endearing if somewhat pathetic natives. Soon after, Diderot illustrates in his *Supplément au voyage de Bougainville* that the Tahitians, far from representing an eccentric oddity in the history of social mores, were actually more civilized than the barbarians who had come to civilize them. Rather than in Persia, Peru, or Tahiti, there was a growing suspicion that the Other resided somehow "at home," among the French. It was the libertine novel in general—and *Dangerous Liaisons* in particular—that took the final step along this path: it placed the Other within French society, thoroughly disguised as the Same.[11]

In so doing, *Dangerous Liaisons* taps into more than specific concerns about the aristocracy, or a more general discomfort about the unrecognizability of the Other; it also draws on a profound anxiety about the culture's ability to maintain the distinctions that were constitutive of the classical imagination. While it is true that Laclos's novel ends in apparent resolution, the satisfaction of this resolution is undermined by the suspicions the novel itself casts upon symbolic operations, especially language. Indeed, throughout the novel libertinism is associated with deceitful language (lies, ambiguity, double-entendre, and "writing" in general), and the problem of language reaches a crisis when the libertines themselves are unsure of what each other means.[12] However, the novel's conclusion can be read as an attempt to restore the transparency of signs. With the departure of the marquise de Merteuil comes a return to order; unsavory libertinism appears to have been uncovered and evicted. The artifices of libertinism collapse under their own weight as the marquise, a virtuoso in the ploys of rhetoric and *figurative* language, is "horribly *dis-figured* [défigurée]" (Laclos, 378). Indeed, she is *literalized*: "her illness turned her inside out," writes Madame de Volanges, "and now she wears her soul on her face." Clarity has supplanted deceit.

This drama of ambiguity plays directly to the sensibilities of the late eighteenth century. The ethics and esthetics of transparency, as Jean

11. See Chapter 2 for a more complete account of this strategy with reference to Sade.

12. The most sustained example is the dialogue between Valmont and "la Merteuil" about Prévan (especially in letter 76), in which Valmont flounders in multiple interpretations of the marquise's letter. On language in *Les Liaisons dangereuses*, see Stewart and Therrien, "Aspects de texture verbale," and Seylaz, "Les mots et la chose."

Starobinski has ably demonstrated in *La Transparence et l'obstacle*, were of particular importance at the time, and involved both implicit and explicit debate across a range of disciplines, perhaps most vigorously in philosophy. In short, the ambiguity that Laclos identified in libertine activity had begun to be recognized as a more general danger inherent in signs themselves.

Just one year before the publication of *Dangerous Liaisons*, in his *Essay on the Origin of Language* (1781), Rousseau had commented on the problem of ambiguity in language. Both in spoken discourse and, especially, in writing, he saw ambiguity to operate like a demon in the system, a small but quirky force that could interfere with pure communication. In a footnote he suggested how this demon might be exorcised:

> Punctuation, which does not have this defect [of ambiguity], would be the best of such means if it were more complete. Why, for example, do we not have a vocative mark? The question mark, which we do have, would be much less necessary, since a question is recognizable from its structure alone, at least in our language. *Are you coming* and *you are coming* are not the same. But how is one to distinguish, in writing, between a man one mentions and a man one addresses? There really is an equivocation which would be eliminated by a vocative mark. The same equivocation is found in irony, when it is not made manifest by accent.[13]

The logical extrapolation of Rousseau's concern would lead to the creation of special marks dedicated to flagging all rhetorical uses of language, and this jungle of contextual indicators would serve primarily to lead the reader back to a glade of clear, unambiguous, and literal communication.

Rousseau demonstrates in this passage a nascent awareness of the problem within language. Long perceived as a "faithful" representation of the world it describes, language begins in the late eighteenth century to lose philosophical prestige. Quite specifically, the growing suspicion that language could *distort* what it designates threatened to place lan-

---

13. *Essai sur l'origine des langues*, 12. For a discussion of part of this passage, see Jacques Derrida, *De la grammatologie*, 157–62. Interestingly, Ferdinand de Saussure, a century and a half after Rousseau, also discussed the advantages of a minutely detailed writing, though he limited its usefulness to science (see discussion in *De la grammatologie*, 57–58).

guage itself on a par with fiction, which would have predictable consequences: if the understanding and disabling of symbolic constructions go hand in hand, then language itself, the vehicle of philosophy, risked being emptied of its power.

The defense of language undertaken by Rousseau and others took a sensible tack: it attempted to quarantine the linguistic problem. As long as symbolic distortions could be identified and contained, the myth of pure designation might survive. Thus one finds in late classical thought a widespread denigration of those elements of language whose ruses could be detected and defused; these expressions were to be categorized under the heading of rhetoric, of figurative language. Language whose distortions eluded detection consequently belonged to a more privileged class: the literal.

Paradoxically, while literalness and transparency were, according to many eighteenth-century thinkers,[14] the points toward which language *evolved*, its origins had been somewhat less noble. Considerable consensus asserted the *figurative* nature of language's beginnings. César Dumarsais, for example, one of the grammarians of the *Encyclopédie*, took his cue from ancient hieroglyphics: "language, if one judges by the monuments of Antiquity, . . . was first necessarily *figurative*, sterile, and crude."[15] Rousseau, in his essay on language, suggested that man's first word for his fellow, inspired by fear, must have been the hyperbolic cry, "giant!"; only later could this initial overreaction be "corrected" by the intervention of calm reason (Rousseau, *Essai,* 47). Gradually, however, civilization would seem to have weaned language from its unsavory origins. Figures, which had begun as the essence of language, were to end up as pure accessories. Dumarsais writes, "Moreover, figures, after having sprung originally from nature, from the limits of a simple language and from the crudeness of ideas, then contributed to the embellishment of speech, just as clothes, which one first devised because of the need to cover oneself, have with time become decorative" (*Encyclopédie,* 6:766b).

Accordingly, Dumarsais presumed that the sophistication of a language could be measured in inverse proportion to its reliance on figures. Taking

---

14. Michel Foucault, *Les mots et les choses,* 92–107; Chomsky cites Leibniz's claim that "les langues sont le meilleur miroir de l'esprit humain" (29); see also Derrida, "White Mythology."

15. "Figure," in Diderot, *Encyclopédie,* 6:765b. Authors of articles in the *Encyclopédie* will be identified when possible.

the example of Hebrew, he showed it to be "the most poorly endowed of eastern languages" (*Encyclopédie,* 6:766a).[16] Hebrew's "deficiency" in nouns (the ideal language would present one noun to denote each thing[17]) forces it to resort extensively to metaphorical and metonymical usage: "This is why the Hebraic language expresses different things by the same word, or the same thing by several synonyms. When expressions do not entirely correspond to one's ideas, as often happens when one uses an inferior language, one necessarily attempts to express oneself by repeating one's thoughts in other terms, just as a person who is cramped in the space he has continually looks for a more comfortable position" (*Encyclopédie,* 6:766a).

One of Dumarsais's colleagues, Voltaire, asserted that there was no excuse for such cramped, ungainly usage in French, for Voltaire's mother tongue was held by many to be the most universal and "highly developed" language, offering turns of phrase to suit every occasion. Clearly Voltaire was not "against" rhetoric; indeed, the magisterial figures of a book like *Candide* are so many examples to the contrary. However, Voltaire sees the teeming figures in *Candide* as deliberate, ornamental, and, above all, clearly identifiable as figures. "Problems" arise when figurative and literal language bleed into each other: meaning becomes messy. Out of this linguistic chaos come communicational interference and misfires. Accordingly, in the article "Langues" of his *Dictionnaire philosophique,* Voltaire complained at length about *misuses* of the French language, resulting primarily from a writer's ignorance and sloth:

> Good writers work to beat back those corrupt expressions that the ignorance of the common man first makes fashionable, and which, adopted by bad authors, next find their way into newspapers and public writings. Thus, from the Italian word *celata,* which means *helm, helmet, head gear,* French soldiers in Italy created the word *salade;* so that when one said *he had his salad,* no one knew if the person spoken of had had his helmet or a

16. "Figure," 766a; Dumarsais was not alone in this accusation. Herder and even Renan after him both link the "imperfection" of Hebrew to its emphasis on passion and the senses—those primitive elements that gave rise to figurative language. See Ernest Renan, "De l'origine du language," part II, *La Liberté de Penser* (1848), 2:65.

17. "There ought to be as many nouns as there are things to name" (Foucault, *Les mots et les choses,* 112). See also Swiggers, "La théorie linguistique des Encyclopédistes," 342–45.

bunch of lettuce.... It is only by lack of imagination that people adapt the same expression for a hundred different ideas. It is a laughable ineptitude not to have known how to express otherwise *an arm of the sea, the arm of a scale, the arm of a chair*; there is also mental laziness in saying *the head of a nail, the head of an army*. (3:568)

Indeed, at a time when words were presumed to be potentially equal in number to the things they designated (Foucault, *Les Mots et les choses*, 112), Voltaire's complaint of the multiplication of meanings seems well founded. Expressions such as *the head of a nail* divert words from what Voltaire saw as their "proper" meaning.

But what was this elusive "proper" usage? Like many of the *philosophes*, Voltaire had placed the whole of rhetoric under the general figure of catachresis, of "misuse."[18] Although this figure was generally invoked to describe flagrant cases like "ferrer [un cheval] d'argent"[19] and "aller à cheval sur un balai"[20] (Dumarsais, *Tropes*, 52–53), Voltaire showed, as cited above, how it could be extended to include the relatively banal instances of salads and nail heads. His complaint revolved around the notion that these expressions had been "tropified," turned away from their "proper" usage. That Voltaire never specified just what the proper applications of these words might be suggests they were too obvious to warrant illustration: since nails cannot have heads, "tête" is presumably reserved for more anthropomorphic forms, designating what sits atop Voltaire's shoulders; "salade," on the other hand, should only refer to a collection of greens on a plate. Thus one could again align Voltaire with Dumarsais, who asserted that a word is used "properly" when "it is used to evoke in the mind the complete idea that original usage intended it to signify" ("Mot," in *Encyclopédie*, 10:752b): literality equals origins, priority.

As is often the case in eighteenth-century thought, however, the appeal to origins creates more difficulties than it resolves. Never mind that it remains unclear whether Voltaire would linguistically behead less anthropomorphic entities (can dogs have heads? can worms?); what is

18. Dumarsais, who puts catachresis at the head of his list, states that, "cette figure règne en quelque sorte sur toutes les autres figures."
19. "To shoe a horse with silver"; the catachresis derives from the French for "to shoe" (*ferrer*), which presupposes the use of *iron* shoes.
20. "To ride horseback on [i.e., straddle] a broom."

more damaging is that his own examples betray the premisses of "proper" usage. "Tête," from the Latin "testa," referred earlier (although in no sense originally) to a shell, later to a terra-cotta pot, and only later to the human skull; "salade" designated in fourteenth-century Provençal any salty dish. In this concatenation of meanings, just what was the "original usage" that dictated literalness? Voltaire's "proper," literal definitions had already undergone the violence of innumerable metaphoric and metonymic transformations. Moreover, how could *original* usage ever operate as the determining characteristic of *literality* when the *origin* of language was held to be *figurative*? The closer one looks, the more the determination of proper, literal usage becomes itself a "real" salad, *une vraie "salade"* in the colloquial, "figurative" sense: a confused mess.

This fealty to the literal, practiced by such Enlightenment thinkers as Locke, Rousseau, and Voltaire (Diderot's case is less clear),[21] stood on remarkably shaky ground. With the literal constantly threatening to turn into its opposite, the need for a strict policing of limits was paramount. Figures had to be kept in line. Dumarsais asserted that, "Above all they must be clear and simple, and they must come to mind naturally. They are to be put in use only at the appropriate time and place" (*Tropes*, 39–40). There is, then, a time and place for rhetoric, and when basic rules of conduct are not observed, there is cause for scandal. Such a position is hardly unusual for the time; Paul de Man detected it in Locke's treatment of metaphor as well, where figures are cast in remarkably similar terms.[22]

Voltaire, in the *Dictionnaire philosophique*, went further than Locke by accusing rhetoric not just of scandal, but of violence. When not properly employed or monitored, the figure *mutilates* that of which it speaks: "We speak of . . . *figurative style* to indicate those metaphorical expressions which depict [*figurent*] those things of which we speak, and which *disfigure* [*défigurent*] them when the metaphors are not apt" ("Figure," 3:131). So, useful for providing imagery that is "gay," "noble,"

21. Diderot's emphasis on gesture in the theater (as well as in the plastic arts) promotes the efficacy of illusion, encouraging emotion over intellect (see *Le parodoxe sur le comédien, Le neveu de Rameau*, in *Oeuvres*).

22. "[L]ike a woman, which it resembles ("like the fair sex"), [rhetoric] is a fine thing as long as it is kept in its proper place. Out of place, among the serious affairs of men . . . it is a disruptive scandal—like the appearance of a real woman in a gentlemen's club where it would only be tolerated as a picture, preferably naked (like the image of Truth), framed and hung on the wall" (de Man, "Metaphor," 15–16).

and "sublime" ("Figure," in *Encyclopédie* 6:766b), figures were not without their dangers, and they threatened to undermine the literal. The very vocabulary suggested quite menacing transgressions: "trope" derives from the Greek word for "to turn," and was seen as the diversion of words from their proper usage; "metaphor" evokes "to carry across" (*metaphorein*), and occurred when words crossed their ordinary boundaries. Like other nemeses of classical thought (such problematic entities as the insane, the androgynous, the vegetal animal),[23] rhetoric committed undesirable, sometimes unspeakable transgressions.

In short, the price of figurality is eternal vigilance: figures must be controlled. Inaugurated, in Rousseau's view, by the first cry of "giant!" figures had *become* just such a giant, a monstrous presence, a kind of unruly force that Rousseau's special punctuation—like the innumerable Lilliputian cords restraining Gulliver—would hold in place.

Dumarsais facilitated the neutralization of rhetoric by his manual on tropes. Since the cataloguing of figures outlined their individual characteristics, the "special trait [*caractère propre*] that constitutes their difference" ("Figure," in *Encyclopédie,* 6:767a), Dumarsais's treatise trained the reader to distinguish rhetorical figures not only from one another, but also, as a group, from what was construed as more passive, literal discourse. Once the lexical or structural traits that flag a figure had been learned (e.g., "like" or "as" for the simile, or inversion for the chiasmus), such structures could be ignored or excluded by the reader, should they infringe upon clarity.

Given the importance of the recognizability of figures, it is not surprising that irony had appeared as Rousseau's particular bugaboo in the *Essay on the Origin of Language*: irony is precisely the *unmarked figure* in writing. While other figures betray their presence by structural flags, irony introduces its radical difference under the cloak of sameness: Dumarsais notes that irony turns its subject in derision "with the same words with which ordinary speech casts praise" ("Ironie," in *Encyclopédie,* 8:906a), and that the "real" meaning is best detected by attention to gesture and intonation. These vocal and gestural indicators are of course not available when irony surfaces in a written text, and writing (as Rousseau warned us) thus aggravates the problem. Just as eighteenth-century thinkers had posited the earliest writing as figurative (e.g. Egyptian hiero-

23. On androgyns, see Pierre Darmon, *Trial by Impotence,* 40–58; on the mad, see Michel Foucault, *Histoire de la folie à l'âge classique*; on troublesome categories in the sciences, see Norman Hampson, 73–96.

glyphics and Chinese ideograms), they tended to view writing and rhetoric with the same uneasy suspicion: both served to disperse meaning rather than transmit it. Irony, then, when found in writing, is doubly dangerous.[24] It masks itself as "proper" language, which it criminally enters, and within which it can circulate "miscognito," neither disciplined nor removed to its proper place. The antithesis of the classical sign, irony points both toward and away from that which it most obviously designates.[25] These are the very qualities that writers would avidly cultivate in the coming decades; however, to much of the eighteenth-century imagination, irony represented the worst-case scenario of language gone awry.[26]

Now, how might this excursion into the philosophy of language help us understand the narrative force of *Dangerous Liaisons*? We have seen how the classical imagination privileged literal over figurative usage. The former was believed to serve purely to designate, and to efface itself in the process; on the other hand, figurative language alters, influences, and distorts that which it represents. This kind of misrepresentation lies at the heart of Laclos's drama. In a celebrated example (letter 48), Valmont playfully writes to the Présidente de Tourvel from the bed of his mistress, using the latter's wearied body as a writing desk. "It is after a tempestuous and sleepless night," he confesses, "... that I come to seek from you, Madame, a calmness which I need, but do not hope yet to enjoy." Waxing ever more fervent, Valmont continues, "Never have I had such pleasure in writing you; never has this activity given rise to such a sweet and yet so acute emotion. Everything seems to heighten my bliss: I am breathing the air of voluptuousness; the very table upon which I write to you, dedicated for the first time to this use, becomes for me the holy alter of my love; how beautiful it seems to my eyes! I will have

24. Derrida's critique of logocentrism (*De la grammatologie*) thus holds for the history of rhetoric as well. See Derrida, "White Mythology."
25. Irony, in this sense, is not to be confused with popular eighteenth-century satire, which eschews any serious ambiguity. The exaggeration of images in Voltaire's *contes philosophiques*, for example, is designed to prevent the reader from accepting the story at face value. Similarly, satirical drawings and engravings in the eighteenth century regularly provide "keys": labels or telltale quotes promoting the identification of personages and eliminating ambiguity.
26. Nor is this perception limited to the eighteenth century. In spite of the linguistic shift to be discussed below, the *desire* for transparent discourse keeps its hold on the modern sensibility. "Univocity is the essence, or better, the *telos* of language," writes Derrida. "No philosophy, as such, has ever renounced this Aristotelian ideal" ("White Mythology," 247).

imprinted upon it the oath to venerate you forever!" (104). Valmont pronounces an *oath*—a supposed guarantee of transparency—at the same time that he *subverts* this transparency. What good is an oath if ironic? Irony and oaths are diametrically opposed; an ironic oath is a logical catachresis. This discourse, by which Valmont tells the Présidente precisely what she wants to hear, all the while relaying "a faithful account of my situation and conduct" (102), amounts to the quintessential libertine act (as will be further explored in Chapter 2), and one that is repeated in a great number of forms throughout the novel. I would suggest that Laclos's association of libertinism and irony is not coincidental; the one rides on the coattails of the other. The threats they pose to the classical imagination are in fact identical: irony, like the libertines themselves, constitutes an otherness disguised as the same. Laclos's novel then, and to some extent the other novels and paraliterary texts of the libertine tradition, gain public currency and provoke response because they have tapped into a rich and deep vein of general concern.

If stories can often be read as a negotiation of personal or cultural "problems,"[27] then the conclusion of *Dangerous Liaisons* should provide some resolution not only for the problem of libertinism, but also for that of the irony that fuels it. As we have seen, it does, and in an apparently conservative way.[28] Fictions, we have said, cease to be effective when their devices are revealed, and the principle holds true for fictions within fictions as well: when her ruses are uncovered at the end of the novel, Mme de Merteuil packs her bags. In the end of the novel can be read the recognition of her "figurality"; that is, of the ambiguity, irony, and treachery of libertinism. Figurality is to be relegated to the margins, and in the sociogeography of the French eighteenth-century imagination, the "margin" means generally "the provinces," or "abroad," which is Mme de Merteuil's destination. The exile of the libertine restores order by relegat-

27. This assertion has been presented most forcefully by Stephen Greenblatt, especially in "Toward a Poetics of Culture," 11–13. The notion is illustrated by Greenblatt in a particularly appealing analysis of Columbus's diary and letters (*Marvelous Possessions,* 52–85), where the adventurer's correspondence is shown to be rich with rhetorical maneuvers, the object of which was to shape the way in which the Old World could think about—and use—the New.

28. I say "apparently" because it is also possible to read the ending as more subversive: the *lack* of closure (Mme de Merteuil does escape, with her jewels, and thus succeeds in swindling society at least one last time) can be read as evidence either of Laclos's subversiveness or of a "loophole" in the resolution he has negotiated.

ing her to the background, just as the policing of language (for Rousseau, Voltaire, Dumarsais) aims to reduce figures to the status of an ornament.

The Advent of the Modern

Yet just how effective is Laclos's restoration of order? His "solution" for the semiotic instability occasioned by libertinism is itself symbolic, and as such, it remains unstable: it relies on the reader's faith in its illusory closure. But the conclusion concludes with a loophole, a footnote from the letter's editor:

> Certain considerations and private reasons, which we will always make it our duty to respect, force us to stop here.
>
> At this time we can neither give the reader the sequel of the adventures of mademoiselle de Volanges, nor make known to him the events which crowned the misfortunes or consummated the punishment of Mme de Merteuil.
>
> Perhaps one day we will be permitted to complete this work; but we can make no guarantees to that effect: and were we able to, we would first believe it necessary to consult the taste of the public, which does not have the same reasons as we to pursue this reading.
>
> —Editor's Note

Against the best interests of symbolic resolution, the editor makes it clear that the end remains potentially *open*. Moreover, his heavy-handed use of commonplace artifices to assert the authenticity of the letters he presents (especially in the editor's preface, but also by the nesting of documentary notes throughout) makes his use of language appear distinctly untrustworthy, almost "libertine" itself. The "transparency" to which the novel returns us is questionable at best, and to the extent that the narrative calls attention (intentionally, I would suggest) to the problem of its own fictionality, it has undercut (deliberately) that aspect of its effect.

I would argue that *Dangerous Liaisons* both discusses and illustrates the collapse of stable semiotics, and is symptomatic of the disintegration of the classical imagination. This is certainly not to say that the "shiftiness" of figurality was new to language, or even to the eighteenth-century understanding of it. However, according to the classical imagination, this shiftiness was incidental; never had it been thought that figurality might prove *constitutive* of language, its sine qua non. The intimation that signs could not transparently reproduce reality (i.e., that there is no such thing as the truly "literal"), but rather that they *always* symbolically alter it (i.e., that representation is *always* figurative), constituted a first impulse toward modernity. Indeed, if the classical imagination can be characterized by its belief in stable and transparent signs, an essential component of the classical esthetics of mimesis, the hallmark of the modern imagination is its skepticism regarding signs, its distrust of the legitimacy of symbolic solutions. The modern deliberately elaborates ambiguity and irony, the nemeses of classical thought (Rorty, *Contingency, Irony, and Solidarity,* 3–5).

However, the shift from the classical to the modern was not neat. Various attempts in recent years to renovate historical periodization, such as those undertaken and inspired by Foucault, Barthes, and Kristeva have situated the inauguration of the modern in the late nineteenth century, identifying its literary manifestation with such figures as Mallarmé and Lautréamont.[29] Yet I would argue that if the classical imagination enjoyed its last hurrah in the middle of the eighteenth century, then figures like Mallarmé and Lautréamont, writing in the last third of the nineteenth century, do not announce the *advent* of the modern so much as they mark its *institutionalization*.[30] Of special interest to us is the epistemological gap: what lies *between*, say, Rousseau and Mallarmé, in the decades *separating* the demise of the classical and the institutionalization of the modern?

I shall argue that this extremely turbulent period in French history, stretching roughly from the Revolution through the end of the Second Empire, marks the transition to the modern. If the transition spanned decades, it is because it was caught in a kind of epistemological double bind. On the one hand, the country had been met, as we shall see below, with a staggering series of social and political redefinitions, changes of

29. See Foucault, *Les Mots et les choses,* 47–50, 119; Barthes, *S/Z*; Kristeva, *Révolution du language poétique.*

30. A recent study on the ornamental arts in the nineteenth century offers an excellent illustration of this institutionalization. Rae Beth Gordon demonstrates that by the late nineteenth century heated debates on what constituted "ornamentation" (and thus background or accessory) and what constituted "subject" (or foreground) had ended by conflating the two (*Ornament, Fantasy, and Desire in Nineteenth-Century French Literature*). The debate mirrors the one I sketched above on figurality, the ornamental qualities of which were admired, as long as they did not interfere with the textual "foreground."

such scope that symbolic resolutions would be expected to be of great use. On the other hand, the central "problem" a flagging classical imagination needed to resolve symbolically was precisely that of the inadequacy of symbolic resolutions.

Cultural Redefinition

It is impossible, in the scope of this chapter, to do more than allude to the sweeping and repeated redefinitions that began in France in the 1790s. Especially during the Revolution, the constant manipulation of language and symbols for political aims contributed to a general sense of disorientation. Indeed, as has been heavily documented, language itself became one of the prime sites of the struggle for political power during the latter part of the eighteenth century, and the actions taken by the revolutionary powers were to have a profound impact on the perceived relationship between words and things. Sandy Petrey has demonstrated one of the most radical features of the Revolution, which was its exploitation of speech acts (in the Austinian sense): in contrast to the classical use of words to describe and classify a supposedly preexisting reality, the Third Estate apparently reversed the process when it "created" a referent, the National Assembly, by an act of naming.[31] The opposite also occurred, when changes in the referential world rendered certain indices obsolete: in 1793 the word "king" ceased, for many of the French, to serve as a legitimate designation.

In other cases, the same symbol could join incompatible referents. One of the best examples of this phenomenon can be found in the revolutionary appropriation of the image of Hercules and the Hydra (or other monsters), an image nearly ubiquitous in the iconography of the Revolution, yet exploited by many different and incompatible parties.[32] Thus one image (Fig. 1) depicts the Hydra as the aristocracy being slain

31. Petrey, 17–51. However, Petrey also shows how the "speech act" is itself less performative than descriptive. He suggests that the creation of the National Assembly consisted of naming a body that *already* had implicit public support.

32. On the "uncommon" uses of commonplace, see Frank Paul Bowman, *French Romanticism*. On the uses to which the image of Christ is put, for example, Bowman concludes, "Eventually, everyone in nineteenth-century France gets compared to Jesus" (24). The same might be said of the image of Hercules during the Revolution. On the development of herculean imagery, see Hunt, *Politics, Culture, and Class,* chap. 3.

Fig. 1. "Le Despotisme terrassé" (Photo, Bibliothèque Nationale, Paris)

by the herculean force of the civilian militia. In another (Fig. 2) the Hydra has become the endlessly proliferating taxes exacted by the ancien régime. Another subtle transformation replaces the anonymous members of the Third Estate with the specific faction of the Mountain (Fig. 3). By the turbulent year of 1792, however, the Hydra has been redefined to portray the factious French people themselves: France crushes the heads of internal discord under her foot (Fig. 4). In the meantime, counterrevolutionary forces recycled the same motif, inverting the terms: in Figure 5, Hercules, now siding with the aristocrats, combats the monster of the revolutionary constitution. The Hercules motif is also employed to depict the heroism of the French people before the repressive forces of the European coalition (Fig. 6). Finally, in an image revelatory of the Revolution's awkward redefinition of the feminine, one finds Hercules depicted as the female allegory of Freedom, crushing the heads of despotism (Fig. 7).

The multiple redefinitions of Hercules served eventually to strip the image of any obvious, "literal" referent. Likewise, the rewriting of certain sign-referent relationships, such as the renaming of the regal Louis XVI as "citoyen Capet," can be seen to contribute to the destabilization of a

Fig. 2.   "A bas les impôts" (Photo, Bibliothèque Nationale, Paris)

linguistic "code." Recent studies have suggested that the sweeping lexical changes legislated by the revolutionary government severely disoriented the public, presumably by its intense and repeated disruption of what had been a relatively stable semiotic system. Thus the institution of the revolutionary calendar, the adoption of the metric system, and the banishment of the formal "vous" defamiliarized the way the French defined basic elements of the world around them.[33] Furthermore, certain words, although scratched from the revolutionary lexicon, retained dangerously modified referents: *Monsieur*, supplanted by the more egalitarian *citoyen*, had no official referent other than the political leanings of the speaker. Likewise, items as mundane as the clothes one wore or the newspaper one read had

33. See Sandy Petrey, *Realism and Revolution,* 46–49; and Lynn Hunt, *Politics, Culture, and Class in the French Revolution,* chap. 1. Both Petrey and Hunt refer to Ferdinand Brunot's volumes on lexical changes during the Revolution in *Histoire de la langue française.*

Fig. 3.   "Hercule terrasse l'hydre de Lerne" (Photo, Bibliothèque Nationale, Paris)

Fig. 4.   "Unité" (Photo, Bibliothèque Nationale, Paris)

Fig. 5.   "Nous verrons qui l'emportera" (Photo, Bibliothèque Nationale, Paris).
Hercules is identifiable by his club, his iconographic trademark in prints of the
period.

turned into potentially dangerous political signs (Hunt, *Politics, Class,
and Culture,* chap. 2). Like the worthless *assignats* the revolutionary
government printed as currency, words were in constant danger of being
devalued—or worse, reevaluated: today's show of patriotism could to-
morrow lead to the scaffold. During the years of the Terror, language had
become, in a very real sense, a matter of life and death.[34]

Linguistic modification is not, of course, a phenomenon limited to the
period of revolutionary France. The link between signs and referents is
after all merely conventional, and conventions are subject to change.
However, during the era of the Revolution, when repeated and sweeping
symbolic shifts affected nearly every aspect of daily life, it would be
difficult to view the volume of changes as commonplace operations of
fine-tuning.[35] Indeed, James Friguglietti has asserted that "the forces that

34. The anti-suspect law of 17 September 1793 for example, allowed imprisonment for the slightest suspicion of unpatriotic activities.

35. On the scope of these redefinitions, and on the appropriation of vocabulary and images by conflicting groups during this period, see Bowman, *French
Romanticism.*

Fig. 6.   "L'héroïsme français" (Photo, Bibliothèque Nationale, Paris)

Fig. 7. "Liberté" (Photo, Bibliothèque Nationale, Paris). Note again, as in Figure 5, the trademark club. The motif serves to overlay the image of Hercules upon that of a feminized Freedom.

such changes generated were unmatched by any event in European history since the Protestant Reformation" (Friguglietti, 13). The Revolution imposed wholesale redefinitions, ranging from the quintessential act of nomination that is christening, to the secularization of death into an "eternal sleep." Meanwhile, caught in a governmental ploy that had nothing to do with revolutionary ideals, tens of thousands of French émigrés who were very much alive found themselves in the curious situation of being declared legally dead (*morts civilement*).[36] Further disruptions occurred in the form of redefinitions of the people's relationship to the land when the Constituent Assembly redrew France in terms of departments (1790), and cities whose names smacked of the ancien régime were summarily rechristened. The map of Paris was redrawn as names of streets and buildings received new, republican denominations.[37] Other names changed as *ci-devants*, or former nobles, adopted aliases, regularly dropping the particle. In a particularly painful move, regional dialects began their tortuous demise under the auspices of l'abbé Grégoire.[38]

The ancien régime, for all its inequities, had been essentially predictable; the cacophony of voices that ensued, for all their republican merits, were largely incomprehensible and contradictory. Indeed, citizens needed conversion charts to keep abreast of all the changes (Figs. 8–10).[39] Rapid changes in the political landscape, and the sweeping

36. For more on the decrees concerning the émigrés, see Chapter 3.

37. It would be impossible in these pages to give a complete overview of the lexical changes of revolutionary France, with which many readers will already be familiar; here one can only signal their scope. For more detail, see Robiquet, *La Vie quotidienne au temps de la Révolution*; Bertaud, *La Vie quotidienne en France au temps de la Révolution (1789–1795)*; Lynn Hunt, *Politics, Culture, and Class in the French Revolution*, chap. 1. On dechristianization (secularization of death, etc.), see Schama, *Citizens*, 776–79; and Kennedy, *A Cultural History of the French Revolution*, 338–53. On the renaming of streets, see Sandy Petrey, *Realism and Revolution*, esp. 46–51. On the calendar, see Friguglietti.

38. See Michel de Certeau, Dominique Julia, and Jacques Revel, *Une Politique de la langue*. Note the decrees of 22 February and 21 October 1793; the first eliminated Latin from the curriculum of secondary schools, and the second required instruction in written and spoken French. The effects of these reforms are discussed in Brunot, *Histoire de la langue française*, 9:i, 147, 169. See also Bertaud, *La Vie quotidienne en France au temps de la Révolution*, 230–32.

39. In order to appreciate the disruption such changes make in everyday life, one need only consider the resistance met by piecemeal alterations of this kind in our own cultural imagination: the continuing opposition to metric conversion in the United States, or to the establishment of a common currency in Europe; the tenacity of the *ancien franc* in common parlance in France; the confusion that ensued Britain's decimalization of its currency in 1970.

Fig. 8.   "Papiers monnoies et autres de la République Française," with conversion tables for different values (Photo, Bibliothèque Nationale, Paris)

Fig. 9.   "Nouveau calendrier de la République Française..." with explanation of calendar (Photo, Bibliothèque Nationale, Paris). Enclosed within a frame containing nearly every Republican image imaginable (the Hydra, the Bastille, the level, and the liberty cap, to name but a few), is the Republican calendar. To facilitate "translation," the months and days of the Gregorian calendar are indicated to the left of each column.

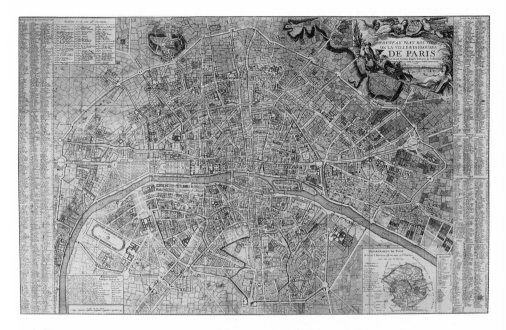

Fig. 10.   "Nouveau plan routier de Paris . . ." Paris redrawn (Photo, Bibliothèque Nationale, Paris). The new map, issued in 1793, illustrates the division of Paris into 48 sections. Some place names (the Champ de Mars, for example, has become the Champ de la fédération) have already been changed as well.

reforms that accompanied them, undermined the semantic stability that was a prerequisite to the transparency the Revolution so desperately wanted to foster.

Meaning was, in a sense, up for grabs, and in the absence of any final, authoritative definition, this disorder led to both social and linguistic anarchy: popular champions of one vocabulary were overturned in short order by others.[40] Moreover, these symbolic upheavals were to outlive the Revolution, rippling through the first, unsettled decades of the nineteenth century. With the Napoleonic Empire there came another wave of alterations: cities already renamed in the 1790s were newly modified; the creation of a Napoleonic nobility parallel to that of the old regime led to a confusion of titles; and with the series of military campaigns came a constant redefinition of what constituted the borders of France herself, as

40.   This factionalization was best illustrated by the division between the Assembly and the Commune, or by the rapid removal from power of the Girondins, the Dantonists, the Hébertists, and, after Thermidor, the Robespierrists.

well as a decimation of her population. Some of the confusion arose from prototypic doublespeak, for Napoleon excelled at cloaking an authoritarian regime in the rhetoric of revolutionary ideals. As if to emblematize the new unreliability of language (and Napoleon's exploitation of the same), the twenty-franc piece minted during the empire bore the inscription "Napoléon Empereur" on its face, with "Révolution Française" imprinted on the reverse. The relationship between words and the things they designated had become exceedingly arbitrary.

The turbulence of the Revolution and the early empire was just the beginning: from the Restoration's restitution of names, titles and goods, to the Second Empire's physical reconstruction of Paris, the already unstable relationship between words and things grew ever more mercurial, until a sense of symbolic instability became part of the cultural imagination of the period.[41] For example, the pain engendered by social and urban change became a capital literary theme during this period. Thus Musset was to attribute the Romantic *mal du siècle* explicitly to social instability: "All of what ails the present century comes from two things: those who went through 1793 and 1814 bear two wounds in their hearts. All that was is no more; all that will be is not yet. Don't look elsewhere for the secret of our ills" (Musset, 36).

Likewise, Balzac's Colonel Chabert returns to Paris in 1818 to find his street renamed, his home demolished, and his wife bearing the patronym of a new husband, whose title of count is the *same* as Chabert's, only *different*, because it is aristocratic rather than imperial. "I don't know where to turn," Chabert laments in bemusement (*Comédie humaine* 3:333). The situation has not materially improved when Lantier, in Zola's *Le Ventre de Paris* returns to the capital in the midst of Haussmanization. "Does *la rue Pirouette* even exist anymore?" he inquires, all but certain that nothing remains of the Paris he once knew (63).

Each political generation introduced its own reforms, each striving to be more authoritative than the last. Not surprisingly, these rewritings of the relationship between the symbolic and the real were undermined by their very frequency. While signifying systems like language rely on convention to establish the relationship between signifiers, signifieds, and referents, the development of such conventions requires consistency of usage *over time*. Dating from the era of the Revolution, massive disruptions in the modes of representation were so commonplace as to put into question the possibility of representation, and to

41. See also Pierre Barbéris, *Balzac et le mal du siècle,* 34–46.

point out the utter contingency of any vocabulary.[42] The situation made many (Balzac among them, as we shall see in Chapter 3) look nostalgically upon the classical period as a golden age of representation, an age for which representation had not yet been problematized.

Acts of Fiction

The result of this extended semiotic instability, I suggest, is that "fiction" becomes, from the late eighteenth century on, the dominant mode of discourse. Indeed, once signs have become so unstable that it is impossible to imagine them as "natural," "eternal," or "essential," nothing is left *but* fiction. Nevertheless, the reactions of individuals and institutions toward the newfound indeterminacy of signs were characterized by symbolic behavior that strove to assert its own authenticity.[43] Here was one of the surprising lessons of the Revolution: although the standard operating procedure of the opposition consists of unveiling the fictionality of the discourse of power (e.g., by undercutting the "divine right" of monarchs), if the opposition accedes to power, it finds itself in the uncomfortable position of having to assert the authenticity of its *own* discourse (say, the inalienable right of the people), thereby repeating the maneuvers of the discourse it has just replaced.

Thus revolutionary reforms themselves came to resemble acts of fiction. By invoking a vocabulary of nature (basing the calendar on the seasons, or the new measurements on the circumference of the globe and the qualities of water), the reforms aimed at re-anchoring signs that had gone seriously adrift. When the government issued *cartes de sûreté* (identity cards vouching for the "republicanism" of its bearer), and *assignats* (bills intended to refloat a collapsing economy), it did so in

42. The notion of definitional vocabularies is borrowed from Rorty, *Contingency, Irony, and Solidarity,* 16–22. It is the inability of *any* final vocabulary to impose itself definitively that Rorty sees as characteristic of the modern era of queasy irony.

43. This fundamental imperative for fiction to "literalize" or "authenticate" itself can be assimilated to Althusser's definition of ideology: a set of "primary obviousnesses," the value of which does not come into question (Althusser, 160–65). See also Bakhtin, who claims that authority attempts to reduce the polyvalence of language to "monoaccentuality"; that is, a single, enforceable meaning (*Le Marxisme et la philosophie du langage,* 44).

hopes of creating stability. However, when the fictionality of these symbols became apparent (as when *assignats* were recognized as essentially
worthless), turbulence ensued.

The tactics of these acts of fiction could be of considerable refinement.
Jacques-Louis David, for one, excelled at the manipulation of images.
Exploiting the revolutionary fascination with oaths, David's paintings on
the subject joined clarity of image with the transparency that oaths—
those of Laclos's Valmont notwithstanding—were thought to guarantee.[44]
Entailing an almost explicit rejection of the rococo tradition developed
by Watteau—a style too closely associated with the court of the ancien
régime—a painting like *The Oath of the Horatii* (1784) restores the sharp
distinction between foreground and background (between "literal" subject and "figurative" ornamentation) that Watteau had blurred. Moreover,
the painting can be seen as a kind of esthetic bricolage, drawing on a
variety of other, apparently incompatible sources for its effect. While it
deals with a classical subject (thus highlighting the military and republican images that were coming into fashion), it does so while recycling
aspects of a genre that would seem inconsistent with the secular subjects
such critics as Diderot had recently endorsed. What reappear, surprisingly, are elements of religious art. It is a genre with which David was not
unfamiliar, having studied under Joseph-Marie Vien (credited with bring-
ing neoclassical style to religious art in the 1760s [Conisbee, 62]), and
having dabbled in the genre himself.[45] Historical painting had gradually
supplanted religious subjects in the salons of the 1760s and 1770s, but not
before artists like David had parasitically plundered the previous generation's catalogue for the emotive power it could generate. While David
drew his subjects from other historical sources,[46] he capitalized on certain of the gestural motifs and stylistic concerns of ecclesiastical art. Thus
a painting like *The Oath of the Horatii* exhibits the didacticism, the
allegorical approach, and the careful delineation between foreground and

44. For a discussion of the phenomena of oaths and denunciations, and of
their problematic status, see Kennedy, *A Cultural History of the French Revolution,* 308–16; and Hunt, *Politics, Class, and Culture in the French Revolution,*
38–47. Instead of transparent literalness, rhetoric again rose to the surface in
the form of metonymic guilt by association. Hunt cites the case of Danton,
"guilty" of being friends with the brother of Fabre-Fond, who had won praise
from the now traitorous Dumouriez (42).

45. His rendering of Saint Roch dates from 1780.

46. R. Rosenblum has identified Beaufort's *Brutus* (1771) as David's most
immediate source ("A Source for David's *Horatii,*" 269–73).

Fig. 11.   Jean Jouvenet, *The Raising of the Son of Naïm's Widow* (1708) (Photo, CNMHS/SPADEM)

Fig. 12.   Carle van Loo, *Saint Augustine Disputing with the Donatists* (1753)
(Photo, Art Resource)

background that were earlier associated (in less striking form) with religious art. More subtly, David's painting implicitly grafts the revolutionary
serment (oath) on the religious *sermon*, both of which try to establish a
language grounded in truth.[47] Appropriating the motif of the outstretched
arm, which was one of the most emotive painterly clichés of religious
painting, especially common in imprecations and such oratorical acts as
preaching (Figs. 11–14), David gives the image a twist, turning the palm
downward. In so doing, he transforms a gentle gesture into one of force.
Moreover, hands earlier raised to God are now raised to the secular substitute for the divine: the state. Symbolized in the weapons by which patriotic duty is to be accomplished, the state takes the place of the church,

47.   On the desire for a gestural art that could serve as a transparent, universal
language, see Dorothy Johnson (93–95).

Fig. 13.   Joseph-Marie Vien, *Saint Denis Preaching to the Gauls* (1767) (Photo, CNMHS/SPADEM)

Fig. 14.   Jacques-Louis David, *The Oath of the Horatii* (1784) (Photo, Art Resource)

just as the crossed hilts of the swords stand in for the crucifix.[48] This technique of thematic superimposition—here overlaying the imagery of the republic upon that of the church—would serve as a key resource of

48. At other times and in other contexts the association between crosses and swords has been made more explicitly: Thomas Kselman reports that in some French cemeteries dedicated to the dead of World War I, crosses are shaped to resemble the hilt of a sword (Kselman, 214). Investing state imagery with the power of the divine is a strategy not unique to David. Both the dependence on allegory (which, although figurative, is a figure that claims to point indexically to a univocal meaning) and the appropriation of religious imagery (e.g., the rights of man as a decalogue, or Robespierre's Celebration of Reason), are widespread in revolutionary art and propaganda. One finds similar collages in David's "martyr" paintings of Le Peletier and Marat. On such "recyclings" in nineteenth-century sculpture, see Albert Boime, *Hollow Icons*. On secular substitutions for religious imagery, see Ozouf, *La Fête révolutionnaire*.

revolutionary art, ritual, and iconography. It was exploited to great effect for the revolutionary festivals.

David's painting exemplifies what I call "acts of fiction." Different from other kinds of "acts" (of God, for example, or magic, resistance, or aggression), but related to them insofar as they focus on altering reality, acts of fiction aim to redefine the world symbolically.[49] Such redefinitions are often of a parasitic nature; they tend to reconfigure symbolic constructions whose symbolicity has been exposed, and whose power, therefore, has been compromised. As in *The Oath of the Horatii*, these acts tend to ride, incognito and "miscognito," on the coattails of other discourses that afford authority (religion, science, politics, etc.). They are bricolages, but not just in Lévi-Strauss's sense (*Pensée sauvage,* 26–47). When they "recycle" materials, it is not out of austerity or a need to "make do"; to the contrary, they capitalize on, and redirect, the energy other discourses can offer. Rather like cathedrals built on the sites and with the rubble of pagan temples, acts of fiction draw on the power of the fictions they supplant—a strategy that itself will work only so long as it remains concealed.

Narrative Strategies

The examples given above show how acts of fiction can be detected in such documents as currency or paintings. Henceforth, however, this study shall focus on literary texts. In postrevolutionary France, literature functions as a cultural collage, a point of convergence for philosophy, politics, esthetics, religion, and popular culture; the density of literary texts offers opportunities for some of the "thickest" of thick descriptions.[50] Furthermore, literature, usually hovering in the margins of culture, often eludes the univocity of propagandistic or explicitly oppositional fictions (Chambers, *Room for Maneuver,* 4–5). It becomes more of a textual marketplace where, amidst the cacophony of voices, numerous negotiations are under way.

Some enlightening work has recently been done on this literature. In particular, Christopher Prendergast's *Order of Mimesis* goes a long way

49. On another view of the way in which fiction can lead to change (by changing desire), see Chambers, *Room for Maneuver,* xi–xii.
50. The allusion is to Geertz, *The Interpretation of Cultures*, chap. 1.

toward demonstrating how nineteenth-century writers found themselves forced to scuttle a traditional esthetic of mimesis in favor of a less absolute model. According to Prendergast, the division that seemed to divorce words from things was largely bridged by a redefinition of referentiality that posited *conventional* meanings—in lieu of any mythical "absolute"—as the only possible referent. Communication is thus made possible by the terms of an implicit "contract" between reader and writer, in which the meanings behind language are essentially agreed upon. Sandy Petrey, in *Realism and Revolution*, takes a similar tack. Using J. L. Austin's speech-act theory as a lever to move the world of realist fiction, he investigates the tension between "constative" (collectively defined) and purely referential language; in the fiction of Balzac, Stendhal, and Zola, natural facts are regularly discredited, "in a world where social facts are supreme" (Petrey, 103). Richard Terdiman's illuminating volume, *Discourse/Counter-Discourse*, deals with the way in which authors confronted the dominant culture in their attempt to excavate within it a space for alternative and generally contestatory discourses.

The present volume means to complement and continue these investigations. Not only shall I draw questions of mimesis and conventionality into the domain of rhetoric (specifically irony); I shall also illustrate the cultural concerns in which these rhetorical gambits are always, in one fashion or another, inscribed. By focusing on the "loopholes" of the symbolic resolutions, I shall bring to light how these solutions operate, how they recycle or graft themselves upon *other* fictions and discourses, as well as how they camouflage their own symbolic negotiations in an age when such camouflage has become exceptionally suspect.

My argument here is that the semiotic instability characteristic of this period subtended much of nineteenth-century discourse. Cast in the terms of a binarity pitting semiotic stability (a belief in the "literalness" or "literality" of the social world) against semiotic instability (or "figurality"), this energetic opposition fueled the literary engine, and much nineteenth-century literature can be elucidated by investigating the approach texts have taken to this binary division.

While the range of narrative developments is potentially unlimited, the number of specific approaches to this binarity have rather strict theoretical limits. In short, and ignoring provisionally the variations that might be envisioned, a binary system allows for four basic permutations: the presence of either of the terms to the exclusion of the other, the absence of both terms, or the combination of the two; see Diagram 1 for a schematic outline of this binarity (indicated here by the terms A and Z). While this

(1)	(2)
	A		Z
(3)	(4)
neither A	both A
nor Z	and Z

Diagram 1

schema is related to the "semiotic rectangle" proposed by Greimas, the differences are significant. First and foremost, Greimas does not explicitly acknowledge the third and fourth quadrants, the logic of neither/nor and both/and (although his "contradictories" imply the presence of quadrant 3), and he thus falls short of accounting for the full room for maneuver allowed by the binary opposition.[51] Second, the configuration of Diagram 1 is designed to reflect the *social dynamics* of the opposition, where the terms of the opposition are not neutral, but rather bear clear social values. One term of the simple binarity is privileged (quadrant 1) at the expense of the other (quadrant 2). Moreover, the complications of the simple binarity are traditionally occulted by society, as represented by the shading of quadrants 3 and 4. These dynamics become apparent, for example, in the schematization of biological sexes as presented in such nineteenth-century works as Balzac's *Sarrasine* or Foucault's edition of *Herculine Barbin* (see Diagram 2).[52]

These schematic compartments, of course, are not airtight; in fact, it is often the way in which a text disturbs or dissolves a simple binarity that accounts for its power, or at least for the strong reactions it elicits. As we have seen, for example, it was a concern for what appeared to be

51. Greimas's model (outlined in Greimas and Rastier, "The Interaction of Semiotic Constraints") has been enormously influential in semiotics and cultural studies, used extensively by such critics as Jameson, *Political Unconscious,* 46–49, 121–27, and Clifford, "On Collecting Art and Culture," 57–60. Although the full discussion cannot be presented here, the "semiotic rectangle" can be shown to be incomplete. Briefly, Greimas's "contradictories," within the context of the binary opposition, are interchangeable. When collapsed together, they present the category of "neither/nor." Greimas does not include the possibility of "both/ and"; that is, the conjunction of the binary terms. However, the detection of this conjunction has been a standard operating procedure of deconstructive reading. For a similar modification of Greimas's rectangle, see Rosalind Krauss, *Optical Unconscious,* 186–90.

52. This schema is not intended to account for the complex dynamics of gender in the nineteenth (or twentieth) century, although it is *one* of the

(1) (+) male	(2) (−) female
(3) ( ) neutered (e.g. castrato)	(4) (+−) hermaphrodite

Diagram 2

inappropriate "seepage" between commonsense categories that had ig-
nited the late eighteenth-century debate on rhetoric.[53]

Such seepage generated spirited responses indeed, and the schema of
binary possibilities can serve to illustrate the range of narrative options,
the four general modes in which postrevolutionary fiction can negotiate
the problem of semiotic disturbance. To the extent that the narratives
we interrogate here address (either implicity or explicitly) this dilemma, they will necessarily promote one aspect of the binarity at the
expense of the others, championing either the literal or the figurative
over its opposite, or joining the two in some kind of "monstrous" union
(the logic of "both/and"), or even attempting to evade the distinction
altogether ("neither/nor").

By the study of four authors (Sade, Balzac, Nerval, and Baudelaire), I
shall illustrate how these four positions translate into four major modes
of narrative reaction, four different strategies for coming to terms with a
nascent modernity. Labeled herein as the modes of collusion, denial,
reconstruction, and subversion, these modes range in their objectives
from the deliberate vitiating of the classical system of signification, to
attempts at damage control; from the re-creation of a mythically "rich"
language, to the exploitation of ambiguities. The strategies are not always mutually exclusive, and it would be an oversimplification to suggest that authors always write in one rather than another; still, these
modes represent four poles toward which postrevolutionary narrative

---

oppositions by which this dynamic can be described. Other oppositions (such as
sexual orientation) would need to be brought into play, after which one can see
in what ways society attempts to occult portions of the binarities, as well as
superimpose them.

53. Though there is not room here for such a discussion, it could be illustrated
that the typical deconstructive gesture consists of demonstrating precisely how
simple binarities falsify themselves and are subsumed by the logic of "both/and." It
is not for nothing that Baudelaire, who will be shown to occupy this quadrant of
the schema, has been the subject of such powerful deconstructive readings.

tends as it works through the problem of rhetoric. Moreover, insofar as these approaches correspond to the social valuations associated with each quadrant of the schema, they will be seen as *socially charged*, either sanctioned or censured, evident or obscured. For the sake of simplicity, then, we might outline the range of reactions as in Diagram 3.

1) Balzac (+) (denial)	2) Sade (−) (collusion)
3) Nerval ( ) (reconstruction)	4) Baudelaire (+ −) (subversion)

Diagram 3

Close reading reveals how the positions in Diagram 3 subtly manifest themselves within texts, even fueling to a great extent certain narrative developments. Thus, for example, the marquis de Sade, operating at the heart of both political and semiotic disruption, can be seen to precipitate the collapse of classical semiotics in his *roman d'éducation, La Philosophie dans le boudoir*. Here libertinism extends far beyond a democratization of love; rather, riding on the coattails of a new definition of nature, Sade colludes with the forces of entropy, working to effect an endless dissemination of meaning. This focus on pure figurality, on a kind of anarchy of meaning, takes the ethical form of libertinism. Sade dissolves social bonds and effectively short-circuits communicative discourse. The "philosophy" of the bedroom consists of subverting the very notions of thought and centered subjects that subtended classical philosophy. Working in the domain of pure figurality, however, Sade's reaction is visible and explicit, and is therefore subject to the violent and total repression with which both Sade and his work were to meet.

Balzac, on the other hand, will represent the mode of denial, and the sheer volume of his work is a tribute to the urgency of his attempt to recover a kind of semiotic integrity. Although "denial" implies a negative response, Balzac's position is positively charged in a society seeking stability. *La Comédie humaine* works, therefore, not only to document but also to *reverse* the slippage of signs. *Le Colonel Chabert* and *César Birotteau*, in particular, reveal the elaborate efforts Balzac undertakes to prop up the literal, to "re-validate" the fictions of the classical imagination through an appropriation of the discourse of science. In the end his own narrative legerdemain, rhetorical in essence, can be seen as symptomatic of the very ill he has detected and tried to conceal.

More complicated (and problematic) than Balzac's approach, Nerval's response to the unreliability of signs consists, paradoxically, of attempting to create narratives that lead *beyond* language, to reduce the distance between reading and experience. I refer to this attempt to restore the immediacy of experience as the mode of reconstruction. In this mode, Nerval works to transcend difficulties of language. From the *Voyage en Orient* to *Aurélia*, Nerval's narrators adopt the role of the translator—of languages, cultures, and psychic states. Their assumption of this role invests them with considerable authority: the translator always occupies a privileged position, straddling the line between sameness and difference. Here the Nervalian narrator unveils before the reader the secret codes of otherness; more important, though, they help the reader *experience* this otherness. In his encounters with the supreme otherness that is madness, Nerval retains the linguistic metaphor, infusing it with the authority of medical discourse. In *Aurélia* in particular, he undertakes to initiate the reader to his personal discourse of plenitude, a plenitude that can only exist *outside* of language, thereby subtracting itself from concerns of figurality altogether.

Finally, Baudelaire will exemplify the duplicitous mode of subversion. After the court case against the *Les Fleurs du mal*, Baudelaire refined his esthetics of corrosive irony, operating in the blind spot of dominant discourse. In *Le Spleen de Paris*, working under the cover of cliché and commonplace, he shows how authority's attempts to conceal its own fictionality can be exploited and undermined, in places and ways one would least expect. Baudelaire writes on double registers, maintaining a discourse that functions simultaneously on the literal and figurative levels, thereby disturbing the commonsense division of literal and figurative discourse. Unlike Sade, whose assault on classical literalness took place "in the open," Baudelaire operates in the occulted, combinatorial logic of "both/and," which tends to fall beyond the scope of the public eye. It is this duplicity that obscures the political threat of Baudelaire's work—as well as the work of others working in the same mode, such as Flaubert.

Four modes, four authors. Clearly this volume cannot pretend to deal adequately with the broad array of narrative strategies developed over the nineteenth century. Instead, I have abstracted the problem of language as a single issue (albeit, I believe, an important one) from among many, one which appears to have been formative in the cultural imagination of postrevolutionary France. By sketching only one example of each of the modes of reaction I have identified, I risk the accusation of a twofold reduction: (1) the reduction of the works in question to treatises on language; (2) the reduction of the modes of reaction to these specific strategies.

Neither of these reductions is intended. If I have limited the analysis primarily to the works of four authors, it is because my primary concern here will be to illustrate narrative strategies in their richness. The task is rendered all the more challenging by the subtlety with which these particular texts operate. Coming in the wake of the relatively new distrust of symbolic resolutions, these fictions work hard to cover their tracks and to promote the kind of readerly misrecognition that is necessary for them to succeed. Accordingly, the studies I offer here attempt to "recognize misrecognition." To do so, they employ a form of textual analysis that takes into account the text's intricate entanglements with its contexts and with what I have referred to as the readers' cultural imagination.

As the title of this volume suggests, the readings that follow focus on *acts* of fiction; however, it should be evident by now that the term cuts two ways. It alludes, in the first instance, to the way narratives attempt to *enact* modifications in social reality; in the second, it highlights the sense in which these fictions are "just an act," illusory resolutions of certain tensions. Strangely, these definitions, seemingly incompatible, do not exclude one another. As evidenced by the political resonances of the works I shall address, illusions have their force. So, occupying the middle ground between action and its simulacrum, fiction crosses standard boundaries; it is resolutely *both*.

Nowhere is this transgression of categories better exemplified than in the work of the marquis de Sade, where it can be caught, so to speak, flagrante delicto. Let us then turn our attention to the bedroom.

2 Viral Fictions: Sade and the Pox of Libertinism

In Chapter 1 we saw how the uneasiness of the classical imagination manifested itself in reflections upon language. But what possible link exists between rhetorical devices and the work of the marquis de Sade? Do such libertine novels as *Justine, ou les malheurs de la vertu* (1791), *Histoire de Juliette, ou les prospérités du vice* (1797), or *La Philosophie dans le boudoir* (1795) demonstrate the slightest concern for matters of language, or does "le divin marquis" have his mind on other affairs? Moreover, even if language did play a part, it would seem that rhetoric remains on the sidelines. The scandal of Sade appears to have more to do with a heinous literality: going against the grain of any form of classical decorum, the champion of libertinism abandons euphemism and preciosity in favor of a brutally direct presentation of acts that many would qualify as unspeakable. Indeed, Sade's writing seems, at least at first blush, to be a zealous realization of the ideal of linguistic transparency. For all his faults, he does not beat around the bush; to the contrary, he calls a spade a spade, employing a vocabulary so explicit that many of his twentieth-century commentators have resorted to censoring their own quotations of his texts.

Yet, the "precision" of Sade's language (which, after all, consists of nothing more than the inclusion of a couple dozen taboo words) hardly accounts for the inflammatory power of the novels.[1] The violence of reactions to Sade's prose suggests that something other than mere scandal inhabits his language; there is also something that speaks to and inflames the passions—qualities that contemporary theoreticians such as César Dumarsais had attributed to *figurative* language. A shared power thus binds libertinism and figurality, a link best illustrated in Sade's novels by a special kind of "libertine figure" that attempts to address the senses directly, circumventing the intellect altogether: thus can libertinism and figurality be seen to share the rubric of *déraison*, that nemesis of the classical imagination.

Moreover, figurality rediscovers its origins in Sade, reappearing as the *graphic image*, which also often suffered from the stigma of *déraison*.[2] Joining the perversions so dear to Sade with the picturality that characterized the origins of rhetoric are those truly graphic figures, the explicit engravings adorning the editions Sade oversaw.[3] Ranging from a single frontispiece in *La Philosophie dans le boudoir* to a series of plates in *Histoire de Juliette*, these illustrations highlight the shared ground, the common denominator of figures and libertinism (see Figs. 15–17).

Textual illustrations might often be considered ornamental accessories to a text, much as classical linguistics tended to relegate figurative language to the status of embellishment. Yet in Sade, engravings exceed the role of mere titillating ornamentation; they represent the most extreme expression of a discourse that privileges figurality. Unlike the decorous prose of Voltaire, where rhetoric seems to lie passively in the

1. Indeed, Roland Barthes's work on the striptease would suggest that such precision adds little to the text's eroticism; more seductive is the "vêtement qui baille," the text that suggests more than it reveals. In Sade, Barthes points out, there is "no striptease" (*Sade, Fourier, Loyola,* 158; on Sadian language, see 133–34, 148–49).

2. Many theoreticians considered hieroglyphics and Chinese ideograms to be primitive, pictorial forms of writing, the residue of which subsists in modern, "advanced" language in the form of rhetorical figures; see Chapter 1. On the stigma of images, see Robert Goldstein, *Censorship of Political Caricature in Nineteenth-Century France.*

3. These illustrations, samples of which are given in the following pages, undoubtedly contributed to the popularity of the works, a sales strategy exploited by others at the time, including Restif de la Bretonne. Annie Le Brun notes that Sade was thought to have had a hand in the artistry ("Notice bibliographique," in *Histoire de Juliette, ou les prospérités du vice,* in *Oeuvres complètes du marquis de Sade,* 8:24.) Unless otherwise noted, all citations of Sade's work will be to this edition, indicated in the text.

Fig. 15. Illustration from *Histoire de Juliette* (Photo, Bibliothèque Nationale, Paris)

Fig. 16.   Illustration from *Histoire de Juliette* (Photo, Bibliothèque Nationale, Paris)

Fig. 17.   Illustration from *Histoire de Juliette* (Photo, Bibliothèque Nationale, Paris)

service of the literal (and where rhetoric and philosophy are essentially opposed), Sade's version of the *conte philosophique* harnesses and exploits the power of figurality. However, Sade never explicitly couches his arguments in terms of language. Rather, his narrative subsumes the narrow concerns of linguistics under the general heading of *ethics*.[4] Now, casting Sade as an ethicist may seem off-key to the casual reader, overwhelmed by the carnage and carnality so rampant in Sadian tales; yet the tales deal exhaustively and intimately, and often explicitly, with the confrontation between desire and law. Although initially it seems to be a contradiction in terms, Sade writes an ethics of libertinism.

It is here that one begins to understand what might be called Sade's mode of collusion. His fiction does not attempt to resolve the problems of the disintegrating classical imagination; indeed, for Sade this imagination *was* the problem. His own fiction, then, seeks to undermine the fictions held most dearly by the eighteenth century, and they do so largely by dissolving the very distinctions upon which classical sensibilities were constructed. This is why the conflation of linguistics and ethics is potentially so inflammatory. To oversimplify for a moment, the binary thinking of the classical imagination had tended to equate literality with virtue, figurality with vice. Figures, as we saw in Chapter 1, were placed under the general rubric of catachresis, of linguistic "abuse" or "impropriety,"[5] terms whose ethical undertones could just as easily describe what is at the heart of Sade's novels. Sade's onslaught on virtue, on what is "proper," thus resonates in a decidedly verbal dimension. Nowhere is the conflation of language and ethics more apparent than in Sade's favorite target, religion, for religion generally represents both the highest virtue and the purest language. Its main components are, after all, *linguistic*: the Gospel (i.e., the Word, *parole*, logos), the Commandments, and Law (logos again) in general. Moreover, God is presented as the Word that all can understand; He is the Word that means what It says, invariably (eternally): the Truth. This is the very idealization of literality.[6]

4. Jacques Lacan associated Sade with Kant: "Here Sade is the inaugural step of a subversion of which the turning point is . . . Kant," ("Kant avec Sade," in *Ecrits,* 2:120).

5. See Voltaire ("Langues") and Dumarsais (*Traité des tropes*).

6. Although the "Good Word" is truffled with allegories and other figures, these allegories profess to point to truth. Dumarsais distinguishes between "good" rhetoric (that which, purely ornamental, facilitates communication) and "bad" (that which infects clear language and clouds it); see Chapter 1. In spite of (or perhaps even by way of) its figures, religious language promises to reveal a

Vice, then, has little or nothing to do with that handful of porno-graphic expletives peppering Sade's prose. (Indeed, had Sade's texts been perceived as "mere" pornography, the authorities would have been more likely to peruse than to censor them.)[7] Far more disquieting for the besieged classical sensibility was the preeminence of words meaning other than what they say, a trait common to both deceit and figurality. In Sade, such textual hypocrisy results in outrageous illu-sions: pure vice masquerades as virtue; or, as in *La Philosophie dans le boudoir* (*Philosophy in the Bedroom*), philosophy dresses up as pornography.

Masquerade is an essential component of libertinism, for the libertine always wears a veneer of virtue. In fact, the ability to *counterfeit* is the principal threat posed by the libertine; it promises to render vice and virtue indistinguishable from one another. This same unrecognizability is precisely why Rousseau had reproached irony; like irony, the liber-tine is the "unmarked figure," an imposter whose otherness, whose inauthenticity, cannot even be detected. Indeed, one's success as liber-tine relates directly to one's ability to pass for something else. Accord-ingly, duality is a convention of the genre of the libertine novel: in *Les Liaisons dangereuses* (1782), Valmont succeeds with the Présidente de Tourvel in direct proportion to his ability to convince her of the sincer-ity of his declarations; in *Le Paysan perverti* (*The Peasant Perverted*, Restif de la Bretonne, 1775), Edmond studies the art of deception.

Sade's libertines, however, go further. Not content to prey on particu-larly gullible or vulnerable individuals, the Sadian hero strives to maintain a pristine identity for the general public, all the while indulging in the blackest of crimes within a secret community of debauchery. Thus in *Justine, ou les malheurs de la vertu*, the title character passes from monks to doctors to gentlemen, believing herself rescued at each step, for each savior enjoys a higher reputation than the last; of course, she never does more than jump from the frying pan into the fire—until she is finally cooked by a retributive bolt of lightning in the final pages. *Justine* is no

---

truth (i.e., a god, a meaning); libertinism, on the other hand, brandishes an empty, unreliable language.

7. Fragonard's erotic paintings, for example, went to well-placed citizens. Eroticism came under the purview of the censor when it became too public, when it threatened to cause a stir. See Mary Sheriff, "Fragonard's Erotic Mothers and the Politics of Reproduction," in Lynn Hunt, ed., *Eroticism and the Body Politic,* 14–40.

exception: all of Sade's novels employ the device of the libertine's double identity. In *La Philosophie dans le boudoir*, Mme de Saint-Ange and Dolmancé are respected members of society; in *Les Cent-vingt journées de Sodome* (*The One Hundred and Twenty Days of Sodom*), one of the libertines is a bishop; in the *Histoire de Juliette*, it is the pope himself who leads two lives.

It is this duality, this unrecognizability, that makes the libertine the very embodiment of irony. One might wish—as Rousseau had wished upon irony—that the libertine be required to identify himself. Nothing unsettles us quite so much as confronting an Other who masquerades as the same.

Of course, the libertine needs his incognito because he has violated more than his victims: in so doing he has violated the law. Here again one notices a certain resonance with rhetoric: rhetoric, as we have seen, is defined by the eighteenth century as a violation of the "law" of language, of the mythical literality, or logos. *Crime*, a word Sade reserves for the most appalling exploits, is but the libertine equivalent of the trope. For the classical mind, rhetoric and perversion have an implicit common denominator, which is that they both partake of a kind of *deviance*: rhetoric was perceived as linguistic *perversion*. This common denominator is detectable within language itself: just as the figure "turns" ("trope," from *trepein*, "to turn") a word away from its proper usage, so debauchery finds its way around another form of logos, the law. This detour, or diversion, from what is "proper," so characteristic of the trope, finds its analogue in a host of libertine practices constituting a departure from the straight and narrow. Thus the di-versions (*divertere*, "to turn from") manifest themselves in the forms of per-version, in-version (homosexuality), and—why not?—sub-version.[8] Moreover, the vertiginous spin of libertinism partakes of another circular motion, one linking the turn of phrase to a turn of events: revolution.

Now, Sade's personal, professional, and literary connections to the Revolution and its linguistic upheavals took a variety of forms. For one thing, those of his official and personal writings that dealt with the Revolution and its aftermath partook of the same shams and subterfuges he attributed to his libertine heroes. His letters, for instance, reek of the promiscuous language so artfully employed by his protagonists, and Sade shamelessly coddled his correspondents by adopting a tone or an atti-

8. On Sade as subversive, see Lacan, *Ecrits*, 2: 120–21.

tude that is demonstrably insincere.[9] Were it only a question of episto-
lary pandering, Sade would pass for nothing more than a man of quick
wit: at a time when survival depended on maintaining chameleonlike
qualities, hypocrisy counts for good sense. Yet in addition to these personal affairs, Sade also played an official role in revolutionary linguistics.
During his tenure as administrator in the General Assembly of his section
of Paris (1792–93), he participated in the republican renaming of
streets and localities in the *section des piques*, addressing a report on
this matter to the Assembly.[10] Moreover, and most important for us, Sade
published a number of literary and philosophical works linking republican freedom to moral liberties. The most striking of these texts is *La
Philosophie dans le boudoir*.

Published in 1795, *La Philosophie* is a sort of libertine complement to
Rousseau's *Emile*. It presents the sensual and moral reeducation of the
young Eugénie de Mistival who, having recently completed her convent
education, has come secretly to Mme de Saint-Ange for initiation into the
ways of libertinism. During the course of the seven vaguely theatrical
dialogues that take place in her boudoir, Mme de Saint-Ange enlists the aid
of her brother and lover, the Chevalier de Mirvel; that of a libertine
maestro, Dolmancé; and that of a few servants as the need arises. Eugénie's
education will consist of a thorough indoctrination into libertine theory,
punctuated by involvement in a series of increasingly scabrous acts. Inserted within the fifth dialogue is the vast political tract entitled "Français,
encore un effort si vous voulez être républicains" ("Patriots! One more
effort if you want to become republicans"), which serves to encapsulate
the teachings of Dolmancé. The tale ends in paroxysm when Eugénie's
mother arrives, hoping to rescue her daughter; this respectable gentle-
woman will actually be tortured by the artful Eugénie and subsequently
infected with a deadly pox.

La Philosophie dans le boudoir never misses an opportunity to devi-
ate from societal norms. Even the title presents a startling juxtaposition:
not only does the combination of things philosophical and sensual seem
to fly in the face of the age-old mind/body dichotomy, but it also makes
odd bedfellows of political opposites. For while in 1795 the word

9. Sade went so far as to counterfeit documents in attempting to have his
name removed from the list of émigrés (Lever, 484). Chapter 21 of Lever's
biography is dedicated largely to an examination of Sade's duplicity.

10. See the letter "L'assemblée générale et permanente de la section des
piques au conseil général de la commune," in *Sade*, 3:369–72.

philosophie automatically evoked the *philosophes*—whom many presumed to have laid the groundwork for the Revolution—the boudoir conjured up the immorality and debauchery associated quite decidedly with the ancien régime. Popular engravings and pamphlets of the 1780s had delighted in portraying the queen as a shameless trollop, often locked in an embrace with her brother-in-law, the comte d'Artois, or with the duchesse de Polignac. The king was at best a two-faced Janus, at worst a wizened hulk, dominated by his regal consort, all of which suggested that this submission of the male was a perversion of the greatest scale (see Figs. 18–20).[11] The Revolution, on the other hand, advertised itself as "correcting" this kind of perversion, casting women in a more "virtuous" (i.e., submissive) role. Once in the home they were out of politics, except as political figureheads: emblems of the healthy, young maiden, later to be identified as the "Marianne" of the French Republic, became the revolutionary counterpart to the serpentine " 'Toinette."[12]

However, the "enlightened" lubricity of *La Philosophie dans le boudoir* makes the popularly supposed lapses of the queen look positively wholesome. Perversions—which official morality defined as any deviation from simple procreation—abound in the soundproofed boudoir of Mme de Saint-Ange.[13] It is in this sanctuary that the hostess and Dolmancé give Eugénie a crash course on the arts of masturbation, fellatio, cunnilingus, sensual spanking, and more. In addition, she participates in carnal configurations of ever-increasing complexity, and which add incest and sodomy to the rolls of crime; she also learns the joys of coprophagy.

These transgressions of the established sexual code are matched by moral transgressions advocated throughout the novel, and extensively developed in the central political tract, "Français, encore un effort si vous voulez être républicains." Subverting accepted morality by

11. See esp. Lynn Hunt, "The Many Bodies of Marie Antoinette: Political Pornography and the Problem of the Feminine in the French Revolution," and Sarah Maza, "The Diamond Necklace Affair Revisited (1785–1786): The Case of the Missing Queen," in Lynn Hunt, ed., *Eroticism and the Body Politic*, 63–89, and 108–30. One of the illustrations reproduced here is included in the above volume. See also chap. 4 ("The Bad Mother") in Lynn Hunt, *The Family Romance of the French Revolution*.

12. See Lynn Hunt, ed., *Eroticism and the Body Politic*; also, Joan Landes, *Women and the Public Sphere in the Age of the French Revolution*.

13. On the libertine sanctuary, see Roland Barthes, *Sade, Fourier, Loyola*, 15–16; and Laborde, *Sade romancier*, 157–64.

OCCUPATION SERIEUSE DU R.⋆⋆
Car apres tout n'en pouvant faire
Il peut bien bercer celui la,
Le débonnaire.

Fig. 18.   Marie-Antoinette with the comte d'Artois (Photo,
Bibliothèque Nationale, Paris)

Un peuple est sans honneur, et mérite ses chaînes
Quand il baisse le front sons le Sceptre des Reines.

Fig. 19.   Marie-Antoinette as Mélusine (Photo, Bibliothèque Nationale, Paris)

Fig. 20.   "Le roi janus, ou l'homme à deux visages" (Photo, Bibliothèque
Nationale, Paris)

reasoned argument, this document, of which Dolmancé is, if not the author, at least the ardent spokesman, dismantles the fundamental presuppositions of society. It does so in degrees, following the outline of Eugénie's initiation, progressing from the least to the most scandalous positions. And, like any libertine prose worth its salt, the progression needs to be minutely programmed, each act surpassing the last. Thus Dolmancé begins by lambasting the "fiction" of Christianity, arguing that a less theocentric religion would better serve the people. Then, after having made short work of the "impostor from Nazareth" and the "whore Mary" (Sade, 3:493), he questions the need for any religion whatsoever: "Let us have good laws and we will be able to do without religion" (Sade, 3:495). And once he has drawn his reader into atheism by the appeal for a solid legal code, he burns the bridge that brought him there: for, upon reflection, do we really need laws at all?

But Sade's strategy goes beyond the standard libertine disregard for popular values. He seeks to undermine not just individual taboos, but rather the very integrity of any system of values. Both in the tract from *La Philosophie dans le boudoir* and in philosophical discourses in other texts, Sade actually enacts a kind of protodeconstruction, which makes of him a dangerous philosophical commodity. In Chapter 1 we saw how symbolic solutions cease to operate once their symbolic nature is revealed, and Sade's collusion with the cultural revolution consists of just such an unveiling. Thus, once exposed as fictions, social cornerstones like religion and morality stand in serious jeopardy.

Sade's strategy for debunking these fictions is remarkably consistent. Dealing with an array of commonplace oppositions (so commonplace that they constitute the unquestioned binary foundations of classical thought), such as virtue/vice, soul/body, law/crime, natural/unnatural, he is not content simply to invert the terms. Instead, he methodically demonstrates how the "lower" element of the pairs, far from being a derivative or corruption of the "higher" element, actually displaces and subsumes its supposed opposite. Virtue is thus revealed to be merely a particular configuration of desires that are as egocentric (i.e., as vicious) as any other; the "soul" is no more than an illusion created by extremely complicated and subtle workings of the body; law is but a kind of theft (e.g., taxes, tithes, etc.) sanctioned by society.[14] As outrageous as his sexual peccadillos, Sade's philosophical infractions consist of the trans-

14. These are the reasonings that appear time and again in Sade, most prominently in *La Philosophie dans le boudoir* and *Histoire de Juliette*.

gression of the bar separating oppositional pairs: virtue, for example, can no longer be opposed to vice because it has been revealed to be a *special case* of vice, just as law is but a special case of crime. In each instance the supposedly dominant element becomes a subset of its presumed opposite.

One by one, then, the "artificial" laws of society fall by the wayside. Slander and theft are revealed to be advantageous practices (theft, for instance, redistributes wealth); prostitution is to be encouraged, indeed enforced; and murder itself is described as a useful public service (it hedges against overpopulation). In fact, what the tract gradually divulges is that the only "law" recognized by the libertine is that prescribed "by nature," which is nothing other than a law of desire. What Sade calls the "droit de propriété sur la jouissance" (Sade, 3:515) is the right of each to satisfy his desires, no matter what the cost to others.

Too revolutionary even for the Revolution? Certainly. Written at a time when the Convention was charged with revamping a rather Byzantine legal code,[15] "Français, encore un effort . . ." offers a seductive simplicity, but one that betrays every article of the Rights of Man. Moreover, while it exposes the fictionality of society's main structures (religion, law, etc.), it does not offer a more tenable fiction in their stead. The libertine utopia outlined in the tract, which Sade touts as a resolution to the problems he has uncovered, is itself riddled with obvious incongruities. These factors undercut its legitimacy from the outset. Consider, for example, these basic tenets:

> Therefore, all men possess an equal right to enjoy all women; according to the laws of nature, no man may claim a woman for his sole, personal use. The law requires them [women] to prostitute themselves, as much as we wish, in the bordellos described earlier; they will be forced to fulfill this obligation should they refuse. . . . What is felt by the object sentenced by nature and the law to satisfy the desires of another is of no concern here. (Sade, 3:515)

> [However] . . . we will balance the lots. . . . These women whom we just enslaved so cruelly, we must certainly compensate them. . . . I therefore decree that these women, being much more drawn to

15. Sade drafted, for the *section des piques*, a memo regarding certain details of the legal reform. See "Idée sur le mode de la sanction des lois" (Sade, 3:331–39).

plans" (Sade, 3:393). Calmed by her hostess, Eugénie nevertheless protests, blushing:

EUGÉNIE: Oh! But I am still quite shaken...
DOLMANCÉ: Come now, my girl, settle down.... Modesty is an old virtue—one which you, with your charms, should know how to do without.
EUGÉNIE: But common decency...
DOLMANCÉ: Another old-fashioned formality, which draws little attention today. It goes so strongly against nature! (*Dolmancé grabs Eugénie, locks her in his arms and kisses her.*)
EUGÉNIE (*defending herself*): Stop it!... Really, this is no way to treat me!

(Sade, 3:393)

Eugénie's moral indignation is, however, short-lived, and Dolmancé will soon investigate a resistance of a more physical nature. After a few summary lessons Eugénie's own body becomes the testing ground for the libertine theories Dolmancé expounds. Not surprisingly, the tightness of Eugénie's virgin orifices—and thus the resistance they offer—heightens her pleasure (and that of her partners) as she is penetrated by the progressively larger members of Dolmancé, the Chevalier, and Augustin. Accordingly, when Eugénie is taken aback by the Chevalier's girth, Dolmancé advises her on the sensual advantage of such a match: "I am of the opinion that a virgin should look for the largest members she can find so that, the ligaments of the hymen broken more quickly, the sensations of pleasure can reach her all the sooner" (Sade, 3:457). Besides, "with a little patience and persistence," Dolmancé moralizes, "one overcomes the greatest of obstacles." As the young student's initial shrieks of pain turn to peals of delight, Dolmancé's proverbial wisdom is confirmed.

The lessons continue at a frenetic pace; Eugénie is a quick study. In typical Sadian fashion, the complexity of the orgies, serving as a kind of "graded reader" for the pupil, is incrementally increased. The configurations eventually reach a confusion confounding the imagination of the most dedicated reader:

DOLMANCÉ: Wait a moment so that I can organize these antics more voluptuously. (*The actions are performed as Dolmancé describes them.*) Augustin, stretch out on the edge of this bed; Eugénie will lie in your arms; while

I sodomise her I will masturbate her clitoris with Augustin's magnificent cock; Augustin, in order to save his semen, will take care not to ejaculate; the Chevalier, who, without saying a word, has been jerking off while he listens to us, will place himself on Eugénie's shoulders, presenting his ass to my lips: I will masturbate him from below; which means that having my cock in an ass, I will be petting a prick with each hand; and you, Madame, after having been your husband, I want you to become mine; equip yourself with the most enormous of your dildos. . . . belt it around your hips, Madame, and let me have it.

(Sade, 3:483–84)

Moreover, throughout the text penetrations are as *moral* as they are *corporal*; indeed, care is taken to match the violation of bodies with the infraction of moral standards, preferably performing both by the same act:

MME DE ST. ANGE: Eugénie, look at me; come watch as I indulge in vice; come and learn, by my example, how to relish it with ecstasy, how to savor it with delight. . . . See, my love, see all that I commit at once: scandal, seduction, poor example, incest, adultery, sodomy! . . . Oh Lucifer! Sole god of my soul, inspire in me something new, incite me to new infamies, and you will see how eagerly I take to them!

(Sade, 3:467)

Logically, this crescendo of activities should culminate with the ultimate transgression, the final crossing of limits that is death. Yet death holds an ambivalent attraction for the libertine. It is at the same time a penetration against the greatest resistance possible, and the absence of any future resistance. A bit like the tract, "Français, encore un effort . . . ," death constitutes a "limit-case" of crime, a transgression that precludes further transgressions. The libertine thus performs a delicate balancing act, staging the greatest transgressions possible, yet always leaving room for a sequel by stopping short of murder. One is thus well advised to proceed slowly, incrementally, perhaps according to the innumerable gradations of pleasure so thoroughly documented in the encyclopedic *Cent-vingt journées de Sodome*. In *La Philosophie dans le boudoir*, the concern for propagation—not, of course, of the species, but of the libertine act—manifests itself quite simply in the openness of the sexual configurations. There is always a loose "end": at least one body that disseminates pleasure without receiving it.

MME DE SAINT-ANGE: Well done, my dear Dolmancé, but you are still lacking something.
DOLMANCÉ: A cock in my ass? You're right, Madame.
MME DE SAINT-ANGE: Let us do without it this morning: we will have one by nightfall; my brother will lend a hand and we will have everything we need.

(Sade, 3:436)

EUGÉNIE: Ah! You are making me die of pleasure, I can't wait any longer!
MME DE SAINT-ANGE: As for me, it's too late!... Ah! Keep going!... Dolmancé, I'm coming!...
EUGÉNIE: Oh my God! I'm coming too!... What a sweet feeling!...
DOLMANCÉ: Places everyone!... Places, Eugénie!... I'm going to be left out because of all these complicated theatrics!

(Sade, 3:439)

DOLMANCÉ: That was one of the best fucks I've ever had....
MME DE SAINT-ANGE: Hah! You said it; what a deluge!
EUGÉNIE: I wish I could say as much!

(Sade, 3:468)

EUGÉNIE: ... I'm dying of pleasure!...
MME DE SAINT-ANGE: My God!... I'm coming!...
LE CHEVALIER: I can't hold it any longer, there I go in Eugénie's beautiful ass... I'm dying!... Ah! Goddammit! What pleasure!...
DOLMANCÉ: I'm right behind you, my friends... right behind you... I'm blind with pleasure...
AUGUSTIN: What about me!... what about me!

(Sade, 3:476–77)

This semicomical "eternal almost" of the libertine act, the inability to fully integrate all participants, prompts the entrance of new characters, each of whom is summoned in an always unsuccessful attempt to close the circle.[18] Unsuccessful yet happily so, for the closed circle would constitute an ultimate, unsurpassable limit, a kind of death, and it is clear that Dolmancé is not eager to reach a barrier with such deadly consequences for desire. Or rather, he would like to experience the ultimate transgression without being subject to its aftermath. This is why the

18. Ironically, the incremental orgy, which many readers find so *sickening* in Sade, is precisely what makes for a "healthy" narrative. On narrative as the prolonging of desire, see Ross Chambers, *Story and Situation.*

savviest of Sade's libertines indulge in various forms of *morts truquées*, or "staged deaths": in *Justine* one of the heroine's torturers, Roland, dangles from a gibbet long enough to "enjoy" the peculiar pleasures of the hanged; *Les Cent-vingt journées de Sodome* relates further anecdotes of the same genre. Like the infractions advocated in "Français, encore un effort . . . ," these transgressions are fictional, figurative, thus having the advantage of being infinitely repeatable.

Dolmancé, however, prefers a further variation on the morbid theme, more along the lines of "vicarious" death, or death "by proxy": he delights in witnessing the demise of others. He admits to having authored murders in order to satisfy his whims, and he explains in some detail the rights of the strong to victimize the weak. Throughout the dialogues, theory (*philosophie*) has always been followed by practice (*boudoir*), and the discussion of murder promises to be no exception. The application of the theory coincides with the infelicitous arrival of Mme de Mistival, Eugénie's indignant mother. An emblem of the law, Mme de Mistival is outraged when Eugénie resists her commands: "What! My daughter would disobey me, and I would be unable to make her respect my authority!" (Sade, 3:549). The opportunity for victimization is too rich to be missed, for in this single instance are assembled a host of possible transgressions: "Here I am," cries Eugénie as she brandishes her weapon over her mother, "committing incest, adultery, and sodomy all at once—and all this by a girl who just lost her virginity today" (Sade, 3:554).

However, just as a form of execution is being selected, Dolmancé surprises the troupe by what might appear to be an act of clemency: he commutes the death sentence.

> Well, my friends, I, as your instructor, soften the penalty; but the difference between my decree and yours is that while your sentences were the subject of mordant imagination, mine will be carried out. I have over there a manservant equipped with what is perhaps one of the most handsome members nature ever created, but which unfortunately distills a virus and is infected with one of the most terrible poxes the world has yet seen. I will have him come up: he will inject his venom in the two natural conduits of this dear and amiable lady, so that as long as the effects of this cruel illness last, the whore will remember not to bother her daughter when she is getting fucked. (Sade, 3:557)

Furthermore, to contain the infection, the contaminated openings are sutured closed. Mme de Mistival is then *returned* to society.

Clemency? Hardly. What Dolmancé has masterminded is far more libertine than a single murder; instead, a credit to his cause, he has committed a transgression that lays the groundwork for future transgressions. The genre of the libertine novel regularly associates the pox with libertinism, cast as the physical manifestation of a moral ill. (Choderlos de Laclos and Restif de la Bretonne are again useful references.)[19] But in *La Philosophie dans le boudoir* the pox does not figure as the retributive wages of sin; it serves instead as the vehicle of debauchery, the threat of a libertinism that will contaminate others and spread like a disease. Mme de Mistival's reinsertion into society is but another form of rape, one destined to infect another body: the *social* body. In this respect she resembles another entity that, if not *sewn*, is "woven" (*textus*): the text of *La Philosophie dans le boudoir* itself, which distills its own virus. The pox the novel disseminates is none other than the tract, "Français, encore un effort... ," those venomous ideas that threaten to circulate within and contaminate the body politic.[20] Like Sade's libertinism itself, this virulent and viral text threatens to contaminate the fictions of society, exposing their comforting closures as illusory. Itself eluding classical enclosure (quarantine, for example, or the textual equivalent, censorship), the libertine pox delights in penetration.

What has revealed itself is a logic of *inoculation*, the deliberate introduction of infection into a healthy organism.[21] Moreover, the entire

19. Mme de Merteuil (*Les Liaisons dangereuses*) ends up horribly disfigured by the pox, to which she loses an eye; Ursule (*La Paysanne pervertie*) is also infected, and retires to a convent.

20. The dream of a libertine epidemic is found elsewhere in Sade, particularly in *Histoire de Juliette*: "A libertine dedicated to such an enterprise could easily corrupt three hundred children in a single year; in thirty years he would have corrupted nine thousand; and if each child he corrupts were only a quarter as libertine as he, which seems more than likely, and if each generation were to follow, at the end of thirty years our libertine, having witnessed two ages of this corruption, will have corrupted nearly nine million, either himself, or by the principles he passed on" (Sade, 8:542); Juliette herself later contaminates a water supply, killing hundreds (Sade, 9:578), and her companion, old Durand, relates how she spread an epidemic (Sade, 9:581)

21. The figurative use of "inoculation" to indicate an infection of ideas or vices appears precisely at Sade's time, at the end of the eighteenth century. (*Petit Robert, Trésor de la langue française*.) The link in *La Philosophie dans le boudoir* between the pamphlet and venom is mentioned by Annie Le Brun (*Sade—A Sudden Abyss,* 168–74).

novel is patterned after this logic: Mme de Mistival is inserted into the public, the pox into Mme de Mistival, the libertine sanctuary into society, and philosophy into the bedroom. The ensuing infection presents the same danger we detected in the philosophical tract: differences that society has a vested interest in preserving are dissolved. As law became, in the tract, nothing more than a subset of crime, so the "health" of society is subsumed by the "illness" that is libertinism. Rather than a perversion of the norm, libertinism becomes, after the epidemic, the norm itself.

Of course, the inoculation is purely fictional. So much the better, for just as the realization of the libertine utopia described in "Français, encore un effort . . ." would paradoxically announce the end of desire, so the real contamination of society by the pox of libertinism would entail the erosion of the very resistance upon which the libertine thrives. The advantage of *fiction*, be it with reference to Sade's utopia, to the *morts truquées*, or to the epidemic, is that it preserves limits at the same time that it satisfies, rhetorically, the desire for their transgression. Fiction allows Sade to repeat his transgressions endlessly, which accounts for the repetitiveness of *Les Cent-vingt journées de Sodome, Justine, La Nouvelle Justine, La Philosophie dans le boudoir*, and *Histoire de Juliette*. Far more useful than *real* infection is the artifice, the *threat* of contamination; it incites those endangered to greater resistance, which is the sine qua non of enhanced pleasures.

Finally, the importance of fiction to Sade's enterprise recalls his collusion with the Revolution in the cultural imagination. Here again libertinism crosses paths with rhetoric, that other undesirable pox that the eighteenth century desperately wanted to excise from another body, the body of language. Ubiquitous but invisible, like an *agent perturbateur*, rhetoric instills the subtle fear that another oppositional pair may be dissolving. Rather than a mere parasite on language, rhetoric may be discovered to pervade literality, just as the libertine infiltrates society. And all these threats spring from what was—and perhaps is—the most terrifying aspect of Sade: the despotism of desire. Here another classical illusion, that of the authority of the enlightened intellect, comes to be challenged. Libertinism, rhetoric, and desire thus become three elements of equal status: they all represent that which is slipping through the hands of the eighteenth century, that which escapes its control. This loss of control, the impotence of the classical imagination, is what Sade delights in putting on stage.

3 Politics and Paleontology: Reading the Past in Balzac's *Colonel Chabert* and *César Birotteau*

> Why do we wish that Nature followed different rules for mankind than for animals? Do not all the classes feed on one another mutually, and do they not diminish one another as required by the laws of Nature? Who doubts but that Nero's actions, when he poisoned Agrippine, were an effect of these same laws, as constant as that of the wolf who devours the lamb?
>
> —Sade, *Histoire de Juliette*

> I saw that ... Society resembled Nature.... There have always existed, and always will exist, Social Species, just as there are Zoological Species.
> —Balzac, *Avant-propos*

What could possibly be more different from Sade than Balzac? Of disparate origins, at opposite ends of the political spectrum, and proponents of essentially incompatible literary styles, these two would appear to have little common ground. Yet, as we see above, they used the same founding metaphor for their works: society as nature. Thus can a single image be yoked to vastly different programs.[1]

The fact is, though, more carries over from Sade to Balzac than this

---

1. On the use of commonplaces and images by opposing forces, see Frank Paul Bowman, *French Romanticism*.

metaphor. The Sadian libertine resurfaces as well, albeit implicitly, in the person of such archvillains as Vautrin. Changeable, deceitful, and "inverted" (Vautrin, for example, is homosexual), the villain incarnates in Balzac the same "horrors" that Sade promotes. Balzac is Sade's antithesis; his narrative strives to revert the world to "normalcy" by undoing the havoc libertinism and its like have wreaked. Only order could put such problematic forces as Vautrin in their proper place—and keep them there.

How was this order to be established? In the foreword to the vast assemblage of novels and stories we know as *The Human Comedy*, Balzac explicitly linked novelistic artistry to science, especially to the work of the naturalist:

> Is it not true that Society makes of man, depending on the various milieux in which he finds himself, as many different men as there are variations in zoology? The differences between a soldier, a worker, an administrator, a lawyer, a layabout, a scholar, a man of state, a merchant, a poet, a pauper, a priest, are, although more difficult to discern, as considerable as those distinguishing the wolf, the lion, the donkey, the crow, the shark, the seal, the sheep, etc. There have always existed, and always will exist, Social Species, just as there are Zoological Species. If Buffon could accomplish the magnificent act of representing the whole of zoology in a book, would there not be a work of this sort to be written about Society? (*CH*, 1:8)

Evidently so; *La Comédie humaine* purports to be this book, replete with a cast of social types that rivals in number the classifications of Buffon's *Histoire naturelle* (*Natural History*, 1749–1789). The nearly encyclopedic goals outlined in the foreword to the *Comédie humaine* have led some to underestimate Balzac's undertaking, considering it little more than an inventory of the "species" of Restoration France, a display of so many exhibits from his human menagerie. For many of his devoted readers Balzac occupies the role of chronicler of the postrevolutionary period, and as such he is regularly plugged into undergraduate French history courses in order to provide a much-needed bit of local color. So, one is hardly surprised to read in the words of a prominent Balzacian scholar that the main interest of the novel *César Birotteau* (1838), for example, is that it offers us "the living chronicle of the world of the small Parisian business of the period, and thus a historical document of prime importance."[2] Balzac figures as the first painter of what historians call *la petite histoire*, or the history of daily life.[3]

Yet however faithful Balzac's representations first appear, they are not transparent. Deep within the landscape of the realist novel there lies a threshold between fiction and reality: a character may step off the curb of the rue Saint-Honoré and enter an alley that has no historical referent; an aristocratic protagonist mixes with well-known personages, although his own name appears in no register of the period; or a specific date is invoked to pinpoint an event that never took place. Balzac's mastery of the realist genre depends on pushing the threshold ever further: his precise depiction of the legal, commercial, financial, and other spheres of Restoration France serve to defer the step into fiction for so long, and to conceal it so well, that none of today's readers (save a few literary historians) can detect the exact moment of transition. Yet these transitions *do* take place, and it would give Balzac short shrift to view his novels solely as so many exhibits from the menagerie of nineteenth-century France; his metaphor of nature implies more than the Buffon-style taxonomic description of species.

Balzac shores up the very notion of a stable social classification, no mean feat at a time of unprecedented social mobility. He invokes Buffon and others so that he can tell stories *in the name of science*, even though these stories have nothing scientific about them. Thus he can mention almost in the same breath scientific schools that are radically incompatible: the classical Buffon (1707–88) rubs shoulders with Georges Cuvier (1769–1832), the founder of comparative anatomy and paleontology; both find themselves clustered with representatives of what we now call pseudoscience, such as the phrenologists Gall and Lavater (1758–1828; 1741–1801), and the mystic Swedenborg (1688–1772). Indeed, "science" makes for odd bedfellows in *The Human Comedy*. However, the

2. René Guise in the introduction to *César Birotteau* (*Comédie humaine*, 6:29). All further references to the *Comédie humaine* will be to this edition; hereafter cited as *CH*.

3. Balzac himself announces this as part of his goal in the *Avant-propos*, and signals the absence of such an undertaking in the whole of literary history: "While reading the dry and dull lists of deeds called *histories*, who has not noticed that writers have always forgotten, in Egypt, in Persia, in Greece, in Rome, to give us the history of manners. Petronius's bit on the private life of the Romans piques our curiosity more than it satisfies it" (*CH*, 1:9).

theoretical coherence of this clustering of figures is of no importance to Balzac. If he associates the novelist with scientists of every ilk, it is because he sees them all as embarked upon a common adventure: the discovery of Truth. Dropping names, he hopes, may lend credibility to his own, analogous, enterprise.

But how can fiction "use" science without becoming mere science fiction? Rather than incorporate details of technical developments (as Jules Verne would do some years later), Balzac subtly attempts to employ scientific *methods*, invoking their power to reveal what may remain unseen to the untrained eye. Accordingly, he goes beyond the meticulous description and organization that characterized the science of the classical age;[4] he also pursues a more modern approach. Michel Foucault has demonstrated that by Balzac's day the focus of science had shifted significantly, moving away from the purely descriptive toward the *interpretive* (*Les Mots et les choses*, 275–92). Thus what Balzac hails in the work of Georges Cuvier is precisely his uncanny ability to discern and interpret minute and apparently insignificant traces, a skill he qualifies as both scientific *and* poetic. "Is not Cuvier the greatest poet of our age?" he writes in *La Peau de Chagrin* (1832): "It is true that Lord Byron has reproduced with words some emotional unrest; but our immortal naturalist has reconstructed worlds with pale bones, has rebuilt, like Cadmus, cities with teeth, has repopulated a thousand forests with a few lumps of coal, has recovered populations of giants in the footprint of a mammoth" (*CH*, 10:75).

Balzac admires not only Cuvier's genius, but also the conclusions the scientist draws from his observations. More specifically, Cuvier's assertions that fossils proved the immutability of species meshed nicely with Balzac's political leanings and social theories. Thus Balzac's grounding analogy between society and nature, defined à la Cuvier, suggests that social types, like species, are invariable, class and character to be inherited from generation to generation.[5] Over vast stretches of time, society thus enjoys the same sense of continuity as Cuvier's nature: individuals and freaks perish, but the species survive, destined to propagate them-

4. Buffon's *Natural History* is a prime example of the classical enterprise. On the classical focus on description and organization, see Foucault, *Les Mots et les choses*, 137–76.

5. In spite of his admiration for some theories of the more evolutionist Geoffroy Saint-Hilaire, in this matter Balzac adopted the so-called fixist theories of Georges Cuvier, who posited species as immutable. (See the comments of René Guise in *CH*, 1:1116 n. 8.)

selves and perpetuate the scenes of the human comedy. Under the protean surface of society, changing with the passing generations, immutable forces are at work. For Balzac, the present is always a reenactment of the past.

Like the paleontologist who discovers worlds in a fossil fragment, Balzac sees the part as potentially representative of the whole. But in his narrative enterprise this synecdoche does not simply aid in the identification of types; it also signals a linkage between levels of society. Thus individual undertakings in the *Comédie humaine*, although only a small part of a societal whole, tend to typify events of the highest order and the grandest scale. For Balzac, that chronicler of the quotidian workings of postrevolutionary France, *la petite histoire* becomes inextricably entwined in *la grande*. Add to this his belief in the biological and societal continuity between past and present, and it becomes clear that Balzac's metaphor of nature implies not only the reenactment of the past, but also the reinscription of major historical events of the past in the context of small, personal dramas. And there can be no doubt about what elements of the past are most relived in *La Comédie humaine*: even those characters who had not experienced the events of the Revolution firsthand were destined to repeat them.[6]

It might appear paradoxical that Balzac, an essentially reactionary figure (nostalgic for an ancien régime he himself had never known), should base his opus on a link between society and nature, a link that is, of all things, *metaphorical*. As we saw in Chapter 1, figurative language was the nemesis of the classical imagination, which would suggest an incompatibility between Balzac and such analogies. However, Balzac does not acknowledge the rhetorical nature of the links he makes. Indeed, the whole force of his presentation relies on the link between nature and society being perceived as real and not "just" metaphorical. As always, the creation of a model for understanding society (here it is nature) is an ideological enterprise; and, as always, the success of an ideological enterprise depends on persuading the public that its rhetoric is anything *but* rhetorical (see Chapter 1). The *Comédie humaine* hopes to show that society is not just pleasantly similar to nature, but that it *is* nature, governed by the same laws and subject to the same limitations.

---

6. Balzac's obsession with the repetition of the past can also take the more personal form of repeating events from one's own past. Such is the emphasis of psychoanalytic readings. See, for example, Peter Brooks, "Narrative Transaction and Transference."

The establishment of a solid correspondence between the societal and natural spheres is not problematic for Balzac; it is facilitated by his lifelong flirtation with Swedenborgian mysticism, based on the belief that analogies are not figurative in the classical sense of decorative, but that they are rather incontrovertible truths.[7] For the Swedenborgian, the perception of an analogy suffices to demonstrate its validity. For the mass of Balzac's readers, who may be less inclined to mysticism, the authoritative voice of science serves the function of guarantee, and references to Cuvier, Geoffroy Saint-Hilaire (1772–1844), and others occur primarily in order to lend weight to Balzac's assertions. Ideally, such "authenticated" analogies would shed their rhetorical status and serve as pure indicators, much as, for the phrenologist, a lump on a skull points unambiguously to a personality trait.[8]

How is one to read such indicators? As we have seen, Balzac embraced Cuvier's model for interpreting the past; however, the problem—for Balzac as much as for Cuvier—is that the indices of the past have been obscured and distorted, rendering their task doubly difficult. What has changed the face of nature and society is a series of cataclysmic events, for which Balzac and Cuvier were to use the same vocabulary. In 1825 Cuvier published his *Essay on Revolutions in the Surface of the Globe*, in which he described how the course of natural history had been affected by certain terrestrial "catastrophes":

> Life . . . has been often disturbed on this earth by terrible events— calamities, which, at their commencement, have perhaps moved and overturned to a great depth the entire outer crust of the globe, but which, since these first commotions, have uniformly acted at a lesser depth and less generally. Countless living beings have been the victims of these catastrophes. . . . Their races have even become extinct, and have left no memorial save some small fragments which the naturalist can scarcely recognize.[9]

7. Swedenborgian mysticism is evoked in the *Avant-propos* (*CH*, 1:7, 8), and provides the foundation for the *Etudes philosophiques* (especially *Louis Lambert* and *Séraphîta*).

8. The theories of Franz Joseph Gall (1758–1828) and Johann Lavater (1741–1801) viewed the exterior of the cranium as indicative of its interior.

9. Georges Cuvier, *Discours sur les révolution de la surface du globe*, translated as *Essay on the Theory of the Earth* (16–17). Page references will be to the translation; all translations have been modified.

Balzac has adopted and adapted Cuvier's premise. What has changed the course of *social* history, however, is not Cuvier's deluges and earthquakes, but rather revolution of another sort; namely, the political revolutions that had shaken France since the summer of 1789.[10]

Now the theme of revolution in *The Human Comedy* could be likened to Flaubert's description of God: present everywhere, it is visible almost nowhere. Indeed, few of Balzac's tales deal directly with the events of the 1780s and 1790s, yet nearly all bear the traces of these events.[11] Fortunes have been made or lost, inheritances squandered, alliances formed and dissolved, all because of the effects of recent social upheaval.[12] Consequently, persons of noble descent find themselves among the ranks of paupers; scoundrels suddenly take on the guise of respected members of society.

As Balzac looks at samples of this new society, his first order of business is to describe and organize; next he begins to interpret, to tell us what is "really" at work in situations whose significance may be substantially other than first appears. How, though, is the truth to be ascertained? Balzac follows the lead of Cuvier, who asserts that in the natural world, and no matter how great the distortion, original truths are never entirely effaced:

> As an antiquary of a new order, I have been obliged to learn the art of deciphering and restoring these remains [fossils], of discovering and bringing together, in their primitive arrangement, the scattered and mutilated fragments of which they are composed, of reproducing, in all their original proportions and characters, the animals to which these fragments formerly belonged... an art which is almost unknown. (Cuvier, 1–2)

Balzac subscribes wholeheartedly to Cuvier's program, and his narrators regularly take the place of the paleontologist. Between the disfiguring scars of the surface, Balzac claimed to read the indelible marks of "truth," that is, of origins and the past. "Truth," the *Comédie humaine*

10. The most dramatic reversals in political regimes in France occurred in the years 1789–94, 1799, 1814, and 1830.

11. The clearest exception is "Un épisode sous la Terreur" (1830).

12. Fredric Jameson has shown, in *The Political Unconscious*, how *La Vieille fille*, for example, can be read as an allegorical reenactment of tensions between political regimes.

repeatedly asserts, is not subject to democratic election, regardless of what certain political factions might assert. Adopting Cuvier's techniques for his own study of society, equating natural and political revolutions, Balzac asserts the ultimate stability and legibility of signs.

Balzac's belief in the continuity and integrity of meaning is at the very heart of debates concerning the realist genre. Recent reassessments of Balzac, beginning with Roland Barthes's *S/Z*, have challenged the traditional view of the realist enterprise. Emphasizing increasingly the theme of language, critics have shifted their stance: rather than show how Balzac transparently and minutely represents aspects of a particular referent (the corruption of Restoration Paris, for example), they cast him as the chronicler of the corruption of representation itself, reporting on the demise of the indexical sign. One powerful reading thus sees the *Comédie humaine* as the tale of a Fall, of the "irretrievable corruption" of signs that have become arbitrary, negotiable, erasable (Prendergast, 86). Another, in a similar vein, argues that Balzac recounts the triumph of the conventional (Austin's constative) sign over the absolute (Petrey, chap. 3). A third demonstrates how one could view the Balzacian *roman d'éducation* as consisting of competing codes, none of which is anchored in any particular reality; they serve primarily to "socialize" individuals by making them conform to any one of a number of equally alienating codes (Terdiman, chap. 1).

These readings of Balzac, however enlightening they may be in many respects, teach us more about modern language theory than about the workings of the *Comédie humaine*.[13] What they demonstrate is that even the rigors of realist prose cannot forestall the collapse of referentiality. Yet they mislead us if they suggest that Balzac's prose actively heralds this collapse. The *Comédie humaine* is a text that resists. Balzac does not simply bemoan the breakdown of ancien régime codes; he fights back.

This authorial pugnacity partakes of what, in Chapter 1, was referred to as the mode of denial, a reaction against the disintegration of semiotic integrity. Going against the tide of a changing cultural imagination, Balzac works overtime to demonstrate how superficial these changes are. For Balzac, the corruption of the indexical sign is not only *not* irreversible; it is also incomplete. Rather than characterize the

---

13. However, Balzac's prose provides the ideal testing grounds for theories (especially those of Austin and Ricoeur) attempting to demonstrate the absence of reference.

representational trouble in Balzac's novels as a poison contaminating and destroying indexical representation,[14] one would be better off viewing it as a pox that spreads and disfigures—the kind of pox that Sade hoped to propagate in *La Philosophie dans le boudoir.* However, for Balzac the disfigurement is never complete: although distorted, the true referent remains ultimately recognizable.[15] One of the tasks Balzac has set himself is that of shoring up the integrity of the sign. So, although his *language* inevitably yields to modern theories about the sign, the Balzacian *narrative* strongly resists the modern, holding out the hope for a "scientifically" legible reality, bearing the traces of its own past.

Throughout the *Comédie humaine* this legibility relies on the trained eye of the narrator, or even that of the reader, who is invited to join in the painstaking task of sifting through clutter and distortion, as if unearthing the fossil remains of another age. In order to demonstrate how these principles of reading operate in Balzac's fiction, and to what degree, we will undertake a double-barreled analysis. *Le Colonel Chabert* (1832) will provide an initial, relatively straightforward example of Balzac's fascination with the resurgence of the past within the present, as well as of his entwining of *la petite histoire* with *la grande.* Here the past and the truth (and for Balzac this coupling is redundant) demonstrate their resilience and inviolability. Once the groundwork is laid, we will proceed to the somewhat more arcane *César Birotteau* (1838) for an appreciation of how completely these principles pervade and underpin *La Comédie humaine.*

Nowhere more than in *Le Colonel Chabert* does one see that France's social upheavals have left scars rendering the past almost unrecogniz-

14. The image is Prendergast's (*The Order of Mimesis*, 98).

15. If, as Prendergast suggests (*The Order of Mimesis*, 116), the pun is anathema to Balzac, it is not because it produces pure polysemy. At worst, the pun produces an alternative meaning, one that seems figurative, and whose comic effect depends on its play with what might be taken as the more "original" or "literal" meaning. Moreover, even the most artful advocates of deceit, such as Vautrin, are indelibly marked. Despite Vautrin's attempts to hide the "TF" branded on his back, a suspicious arrangement of scars leave the authenticity of his disguise in doubt (*Splendeurs et misères des courtisanes*, 6:751). Furthermore, the one thing Vautrin *cannot* disguise, we learn in *Splendeurs et misères*, is his *voice*: one's origins always speak. On the residual, inalienable sign in Balzac, see Françoise Gaillard, "Désordre social et ordre romanesque: Une lecture de *La théorie de la démarche.*"

able. Indeed, the title character of the novel incarnates the situation: a Napoleonic officer left for dead on the battlefield, Colonel Chabert eventually returns to Paris horribly disfigured. His wife, remarried to a count of the Restoration, has distanced herself from her own unsavory past, and sets out to counter her husband's legal attempts to reassume his name and rights. The old soldier's plight is that no one can, nor wishes, to recognize him—a rejection facilitated by Chabert's disfigurement, so horrible that one of the colonel's epithets in the novel is *méconnaissable* (unrecognizable).

This articulation of the past with the present lies at the heart of *Le Colonel Chabert*. On the most explicit level certain forces in the novel vehemently refute that there is any articulation at all: indeed, Chabert's wife, and Restoration society as a whole, would like the old war hero to return quietly to the grave. Yet it is this very insistence on the unparalleled strangeness of the colonel's claims that gives rise to suspicion. Chabert is repeatedly referred to as *singulier* (singular, odd), and the *uniqueness* of his situation is key to the Countess's ability to keep him at bay; singular, Chabert would have no role in historical continuity, and his story becomes devalued in a monarchical society predicated on the value of genealogies. Even Derville, Chabert's well-intentioned lawyer, complains on more than one occasion that it is the uniqueness of Chabert's situation that will make his case languish in a judicial system based on precedents: "The legal point falls outside the scope of the code (*CH*, 3:341)," he says, ". . .it is almost without precedent in legal history (*CH*, 3:334)."

But Derville is dead wrong. Paradoxically, what is heralded as Chabert's singularity actually provides the key to reading his duplication of the past. Although Balzac makes no mention of it, Chabert's statutory death had a precise and noteworthy legal precedent, one involving thousands of Frenchmen. In March 1793 the revolutionary government had devised a means of legally confiscating the property of the aristocracy by declaring the émigrés officially dead: "The émigrés are banished forever from French soil; *they are legally dead* [*morts civilement*]; their property is acquired by the Republic."[16] Legal resuscitation only came many years later, with Napoleon's amnesty of the Year X, which added in a note that "The émigré is given back his legal rights [*rendu à la vie civile*] beginning with the date of the decree granting

16. J. B. Duvergier, *Collection complète des lois*; arrêté du 28 mars, 1789. Indeed, far from being unique, Chabert shared the plight of thousands.

him amnesty."[17] Chabert's legal death thus repeats the plight of the aristocratic émigrés.

The implications of this repetition of a past scenario are considerable. Although it seems improbable enough that the impoverished and cadaverous Chabert could somehow share a past with the aristocratic elite, the analogy of the émigrés puts Chabert's wife, now a countess in the highest sphere of Restoration society, into the preposterous role of the *Revolution*, for it is she who has appropriated a man's fortune by declaring him dead![18]

The novel thus presents the reader with two diametrically opposed, and mutually exclusive, tales; knowing how to choose between the two requires a magisterial act of reading. It seems clear that for Balzac the postrevolutionary world has been scarred by decades of undesirable social upheaval; signs have been rendered as "unrecognizable" as Chabert himself. It is suggested, however, that "careful" observers, fashioned after the narrator himself, can ferret out the subtle traces that survive distortion, thus demonstrating a kind of inviolable literalness in language and other signs. For Balzac, signs never exist exclusively in the present, but always bear some trace of past, "original" meanings. "True" meaning, like Voltaire's notion of literalness, is anchored in the origin. The history that always leaves its imprint on the present can be traced as neatly as an etymology; or, to evoke Cuvier once more, can be reconstructed as fully as a prehistoric creature from a bone fragment.

So, Balzac's insistence on the indelibility of history extends even to a past that has been distorted, rendered "unrecognizable" to the unpracticed eye. This indelibility can be seen in the narrator's portrait of Chabert during his nocturnal visit in Derville's office, where the colonel is initially "misread" according to the terms society has applied to him— those of a dead man or a lunatic:

> Pale and livid, his hatchet-face (if one may be allowed this vulgar expression) seemed dead.... The rim of the hat covering the old man's forehead cast a dark furrow upon his brow. This bizarre effect, although unreal, brought out ... the faded quality of his cadaverous appearance. Last of all, the absence of any movement in his body ... compounded by a certain expression of sad

17. Duvergier; arrêté du 6 floréal An X.
18. It is the Countess who requests that the state give her access to Chabert's assets by issuing a death certificate.

dementia, . . . gave this figure a ghastly appearance that no human word could express.

Yet closer examination reveals that the first impression is misleading. "However," the narrator continues,

> an observer, and especially a lawyer, would have detected more and more in this crushed soul the signs of a profound sorrow, the evidence [*les indices*] of a misery that had deteriorated this face, like drops of water, which, fallen from the sky upon a beautiful marble statue, have over time disfigured it. A doctor, an author, a magistrate would have sensed a whole drama upon sight of this sublime horror. (*CH*, 3:321–22)

Such passages underscore Balzac's insistence on the fundamental continuity between past and present, a link allowing the former to be read through the latter. Bit by bit the novel re-creates Chabert's drama, restoring it as Cuvier might reconstitute an era from traces left in strata of limestome. Balzac, of course, does not deal with rocks, although Chabert's face *has* just been compared to stone. Nevertheless, Chabert is something of a fossil, this block of living marble having been unearthed from a battlefield grave. So Balzac, modeling his methods after Cuvier, hunts for traces of the past that might be encrusted in the present. What becomes evident from the remaining clues, those that have survived the ravages of time, is that Chabert *can* be identified. Likened by the law clerks to a figure in a wax museum, Chabert is from the outset a kind of effigy, the authentic reproduction of another figure. Just who that original figure is leaves little room for doubt: the forty-franc piece to which Derville compares him bore the effigy of the emperor, and was commonly called a *napoléon*. Having served under the leader of the *Grande Armée*, Chabert refers to him as his spiritual father, and even talks of addressing himself to the bronze effigy of Napoleon atop the column of the place Vendôme, a statue that in itself forges seemingly authentic links with the past because it was cast with the bronze of enemy canons taken at the Battle of Austerlitz. Were this not enough, Chabert's biography shadows the emperor's: he rises to glory from humble origins, marries a woman of questionable morals (Joséphine had been Barras's mistress) and who, like Joséphine, bears him no children; the colonel's return to Paris follows hard on the heels of Napoleon's Hundred Days, and the final internment in Bicêtre parallels the emperor's exile after Waterloo. As Pierre Citron has noted, Chabert even reproduces his spiritual father's tics, slipping his hand into his vest and tugging on the ears of scoundrels.[19]

These resemblances, which in a literary context would seem to make of Chabert something of an *allegory* of Napoleon or the empire, marks him "scientifically" as a member of the same *species* as the emperor. Again the analogy is straight out of Cuvier: "A species comprehends all the individuals which descend from each other, or from a common parentage, and those which resemble them as much as they do each other" (Cuvier, 116).

If Chabert is a fossil remain, he is at least one that lets its past be read; indeed, one that cries out for such a reading. However, the job of interpretation in *La Comédie humaine* becomes even more difficult than Cuvier's undertakings: Balzac confronts individuals who strive deliberately to obscure their past, to conceal or distort the signs that might reveal undesirable origins. *La Comédie humaine* is populated with such characters, and according to Balzac, they have no place in natural or political history; they are unnatural *monsters*.

One finds these monsters throughout the *Comédie humaine*, the most famous of which are the Vautrin of *Old Goriot* and *The Splendors and Miseries of Courtisans*, and Ferdinand du Tillet of *The Rise and Fall of César Birotteau*. These characters are invariably products of the same cataclysm that Balzac saw as having annihilated other social species: the Revolution. Always described as "unnatural," they illustrate Cuvier's theory on nature's self-regulation:

> Nature appears also to have guarded against the alterations of species which might proceed from the mixture of breeds, by inspiring in the various species of animals a mutual aversion for each other. Hence all the cunning and all the force that man can exert is necessary to accomplish such unions, even between species that resemble each other most closely. And when the mule-breeds that are thus produced by these forced conjunctions happen to be fruitful, which is seldom the case, this fecundity never continues beyond a few generations. (Cuvier, 118)

One begins to understand, then, why Balzac will describe du Tillet as a *métis social* (a social half-breed). Even his physical portrait betrays a

19. Cited in *CH*, 3:355 n. 3.

certain unnaturalness; his face is referred to as *chafouine*, a portmanteau word conjoining (unnaturally, as it were) two species: *chat* and *fouine*, cat and marten. The sterility of such supposed half-breeds is most evident in Vautrin, whose homosexuality forces him to try to perpetuate his kind by adoption and indoctrination.[20]

These are the characters whose success depends on being able to masquerade as natural members of society, on concealing the signs of their monstrosity. However, Balzac defends the ultimate *indelibility* of these signs, which, as Cuvier wrote, "must be visible to all who are qualified to read their history in the remains which they have left behind." Thus even Vautrin, the master of disguise, counterfeit, and false identity cannot conceal all; that the truth always makes itself heard is evident from the fact, as noted above, that there is one thing Vautrin has never been able to disguise: *his voice*.

Le Colonel Chabert presents one of the finest specimens of what Balzac portrays as an unnatural breed: Chabert's wife, the Countess Ferraud. Remarried after Chabert's reported demise on the battlefield, the Countess has blended into the highest sphere of Restoration nobility: she sports the obligatory carriage and mansion, assumes the insouciance and manners of the Saint-Germain crowd upon which she has grafted herself, and even keeps a pet monkey, become so fashionable in the day. But the Countess belongs to the Restoration only in *name*, dating from her marriage to Ferraud. And names (she has borne at least three of them) figure prominently among the props she wields to theatrical effect. Indeed, Balzac repeatedly refers to her as an actress, and to Chabert's "drama" is opposed her "spectacle":

> The old soldier shuddered upon hearing this lone word, that first, awful "Monsieur!" And it was thus all at once a reproach, a prayer, a pardon, an expectation, a disappointment, a query, and an answer. This word contained everything. *Only an actress could invest so much eloquence, so many emotions in a word.* (*CH*, 3:359)

Later, when she lures Chabert to her country estate at Groslay, we see her drop her mask behind the scenes: "To relax for a moment she went up to her room, sat down at her desk, and took off the mask of tranquillity . . . like an actress (*CH*, 3:362). Actresses are those who simply "go

---

20. A process that seems so "unnatural" to his disciples that it drives them to despair (Eugène de Rastignac) or suicide (Lucien de Rubempré).

through the motions," convincingly, if possible, but without real senti-ment; they affect virtues or feelings they do not have. The Countess is thus a seasoned hypocrite (*hypocrites* is Greek for actor), for she has mastered the art of fraudulent signs. Even the monkey (*singe*) she keeps as a pet betokens the emptiness of gestures, the *aping* (*singer*) that defines her existence. What she has carefully obscured is a past that is utterly divorced from her high-society present: we learn during a dra-matic encounter between Chabert and his wife that she began her social climbing as a common prostitute working the Palais Royal. Hardly a transparent representative of the Restoration, as she pretends, the Count-ess instead represents what are for Balzac the worst aspects of the Revo-lution, exemplifying the social mobility and the sexual and semiotic promiscuity that can allow whores to masquerade as aristocrats. In the semiotics of the Revolution, the novel seems to warn, signs are danger-ously unfaithful; they are encouraged to prostitute themselves. In accor-dance with her past, the Countess Ferraud becomes the very emblem of the promiscuous sign.

Yet how are her origins to be detected? In *The Human Comedy* as we have seen, small details allow one to piece together a character's past. In the case of the Countess, however, these signs are actively concealed; nowhere does the indelibility of the past meet with greater resistance than in the Countess's meticulous efforts to "rewrite" herself.[21] Paradoxi-cally, she and Chabert are in similar, albeit opposite, situations: he, repeat-edly referred to as unrecognizable, suffers from the very incognito to which his wife aspires. Nevertheless, here too, and at junctures of prime importance, the past resurfaces. Even within the chameleon semiotics of the Revolution there exists a dose of constancy. Thus the Countess's actions reveal her ties to the Revolution, as in her use of the revolution-ary strategy of bureaucratic execution for dispossessing her husband of his fortune. Moreover, a reader as careful as Derville picks up on the slightest of details. During negotiations with the lawyer, the Countess involuntarily tips her hand: at an innuendo concerning her past, she blanches ever so slightly. "Now I have it!" cries Derville to himself, having divined her whole story from this single clue.

---

21. For greater detail on how the countess strives to rewrite her own story, see Eileen Sivert, "Who's Who: Non-Characters in *Le Colonel Chabert*," 224–26. Sivert also sees the Countess's theatricality as representative of modern writing, in conflict with traditional, institutional writing, which presumes a continuity the Countess rejects.

Balzac implants other, more subtle, traces designed to show the indelibility of the past. If the Countess's marriages amount to an unnatural mixing of social species, one should not be surprised to see her unions result in a kind of sterility: she had been unable to make Chabert a *père*, or father, and we learn that her political sterility is what prevents Ferraud from becoming another kind of father figure, not a *père*, but a *pair*, or Peer of France.[22] Also, the very elegance of the Countess' attire can expose her rather inelegant origins. An outfit she wears to a meeting with Chabert figures as an anagrammatic inscription of her identity: the "pretty hood lined with pink" ("jolie *capote* doublée de *rose*") resonates with the name "*Rose Chapotel*," that name she has sought so tirelessly to efface.[23] Another distorted trace of the Countess' association with the Revolution can be read in her Paris address: the rue de Varenne. Evocative of the king's fateful flight to the town of Varennes in 1791, the address thus associates the Countess with the subsequent fall of the monarchy and rise of the revolutionary government. Furthermore, the name conjures up an earlier reference to promiscuity, and consequently to the Countess' earlier profession as prostitute: the street name recalls—anagrammatically again—the site of Chabert's adventure in a brothel in the town of *Ravenne* where, in a curious foreshadowing of his present situation, someone had attempted to kill him.

Capote doublée de rose, pair/père, Varenne/Varennes/Ravenne: anagrams like these are among the most striking illustrations of Balzac's notion of the revolutionary sign. Like the traces of the past that Cuvier uncovered in mineral deposits, anagrams carry a past encrusted and distorted within their present form; like Cuvier's fossils, they often appear insignificant, indeed invisible, to all but the trained eye. It is Balzac's narrator who provides the scientific gaze, focusing on the traces of the Countess's "true" history, and allowing Balzac and the reader, in the manner of Cuvier, to reconstruct a past that is quite literally "prehistoric"; that is, a past that precedes the story he is telling.

This "scientific" approach, Balzac as much as says, sees through the rhetorical, deceptive maneuvers of such characters as the Countess

---

22. Ferraud and Chabert share more than their sterility; Ferraud, as a former émigré, would have experienced the statutory death from which Chabert currently suffers. In a myriad of ways that I can only allude to here, Balzac shows that Ferraud and Chabert are essentially interchangeable, partaking of the same social "species." The overlapping of these characters signals Balzac's conflation of the early Napoleonic Empire and the Restoration.

23. On this echo, see Sivert, 223.

Ferraud, Vautrin, or du Tillet. However, what Balzac does not acknowledge is that his own appropriation of science is itself a rhetorical maneuver, one designed to give social and political acts the authority of Nature or the stigma of monstrosity. In *The Human Comedy* science has a social agenda: it does not lead to scientific taxonomy but to social "re-classification," putting people back in their class.

Le Colonel Chabert, which highlights Chabert's association with Napoleon, explicitly ties personal drama to events belonging to *la grande histoire*, even though many of the details need to be teased out. Yet this explicitness is not the rule in the *Comédie humaine*. The story of another *mort civile*, the *Histoire de la grandeur et de la décadence de César Birotteau* (*The Story of the Rise and Fall of César Birotteau*, 1838), chronicles the tribulations of a Parisian merchant, a simple *parfumeur*. Here, although science itself plays almost no role, the curious entwining of scientific method and politics is even more significant, relying heavily on Cuvier's art of decipherment and on the notion of continuity of species.

  Extraordinarily successful since his marketing of a popular hand lotion, César Birotteau reaps honors in his small corner of the business world: he is elected judge to a commercial court, appointed adjunct to the mayor of his arrondissement, and finally named to the Légion d'honneur. Elated over his new invention, a hair tonic known first as the *huile comagène*, then as the *huile céphalique*, César branches into undertakings that have little to do with the business he knows: a major remodeling of his home, a large formal ball, and, most fatefully, speculations in real estate. In this last enterprise Birotteau is swindled by one of his former clerks, the unscrupulous and vengeful Ferdinand du Tillet, turned out from the perfume shop years earlier for having helped himself to the till. The investment scheme du Tillet has plotted launches Birotteau into a tortuous spiral ending with bankruptcy. Stripped of his civil rights (a *mort civil*, like Chabert), Birotteau martyrs himself to his creditors, devoting his last days to commercial rehabilitation and moral exculpation. Shortly before he dies his last debts are paid by the profits his associate has turned with the new *huile céphalique*.

  What makes this any more than a petty story of petty affairs? It is difficult to see how *César Birotteau* could be pried from the bourgeois setting it so precisely depicts. This is all the more so since Birotteau himself begins to realize, during his last-ditch pilgrimages to the luxurious quarters of the banking community, just how petit bourgeois he is. Where does one begin to look in a text that, at the outset, seems almost hermetically sealed within the confines of banality? Since the reading of *Le Colonel Chabert* signaled the importance of what lies in the margins of the Balzac's tales, one might choose to focus here on what is arguably an entirely banal element of this banality, namely the *huile céphalique* itself, that innocuous (and probably ineffectual) hair tonic.

So far is the tonic from the center of action that it seems to serve primarily as a narrative frame: the novel opens with Birotteau's midnight explanation to his wife of what riches his new invention will bring; at the novel's conclusion Birotteau's debts are paid by the young Anselme Popinot, largely with profits from the product. However, in addition to this frame, the oil also fuels a principal subplot of the novel. Popinot covets Césarine, César's daughter, and he can only hope to become an acceptable match for her by successfully marketing the product César has entrusted to him. Popinot's existence revolves around the oil and consists principally of setting up shop, arranging production, searching for an appropriate flask, composing a sales prospectus (with Gaudissart and Finot), and even crating shipments himself when his workers fall behind. Though regular, these scenes are nevertheless infrequent. Balzac seems to apply the theme of the oil in the same manner the oil itself is meant to be applied: dabbed here and there on an occasional basis, and especially at the roots, so as not to be evident on the surface.

Trivial, certainly; yet it is this ointment that for all intents and purposes rehabilitates and even resuscitates Birotteau at the end of the novel, resurrecting him from the *mort civile* he has suffered. Clearly the oil attains almost fetishistic status: its narrative role far overreaches that of a minor commercial product.

The surprising importance of the tonic derives in part from the fact that it points to a history all its own, and one that goes beyond the pages of *César Birotteau*. Popinot's sales prospectus claims that hair oils date back to ancient times, and were even used by French lords in ages gone by: "Learned studies have shown that nobles, who prided themselves on the length of their hair, employed no other method; their practices have simply been lost" (*CH*, 6:156). What he alludes to is the importance the Frankish dynasties, especially the Merovingians, attached to hair as a sign of strength and domination. This is not just a Balzacian fantasy. Edouard Salin, in *La Civilisation mérovingienne*, writes, "The wearing of long hair and beards could have a special, almost ritualistic meaning. Among the Franks long hair was indeed the privilege of kings" (Salin, 119). Moreover, the loss, or cutting, of hair corresponded to subjugation:

Other texts suggest that the Barbarians held their hair in high esteem; to cut it was a sign of submission, an admission of defeat.... And Sidoine Apollinaire [writes] in one of his letters: "Here we see the blue-eyed Saxon, formerly the king of the seas, who now trembles on land. At the top of his brow the shears reach not only the first locks, but rather cut at its root this hair which, cut thus at the level of the skin, shortens the shape of his head and makes his face appear longer." (Salin, 118)

On a more general plane, extending beyond the limits of the French Middle Ages, the traditional association of hair with power can be seen in the legend of Samson, his strength sapped when Delilah clips his locks. Likewise, the monastic tonsure (from the Latin *tondere*, "to shear") was meant to indicate the voluntary subjugation and ovine passivity of the religious orders.[24]

The tonsure began sometime in the Middle Ages, but the fetishizing of hair was still current in more recent times, figuring in the iconography of the Revolution and its aftermath. As early as 1780, abundant, well-styled hair was associated with high society (Fig. 21). A popular engraving circulated (and much reproduced) in 1789 showed a wigmaker profiting from the Revolution (Fig. 22), as the new equality of orders was expressed in terms of *hair*: in accord with the desacralization of the monastic orders, he shaves a monk's beard, meanwhile styling the hair of a noble man and fitting a commoner with a peruke, the peruke being a sign of the noble rank and power the commoner covets.

This braiding of politics and hairdressing was not short-lived. The image survived until at least 1850, when there appeared an anonymous pamphlet entitled "Natural Hair, Old Peruke, and False Toupee," billing itself as a "Chronicle of Cochin China from 1830 to 1850."[25] This brief narrative poem relates in lightly veiled allegory the turbulent succession of three "capillary" regimes corresponding to the three forms of government France had recently experienced: "legitimate hereditary monarchical, republican, and revolutionary monarchical." "Perhaps," hints the anony-

---

24. Other examples are not wanting: scalping (practiced both by American Indians and by those who hunted them for bounty) and the shaving of heads in prisons and concentration camps participate in the same tradition.

25. *Cheveux naturels, vieille perruque, et faux toupet: Chronique cochin-chinoise de 1830 à 1850* (Paris: Imprimerie centrale de Napoléon Chaix, 1850).

AU CAFFÉ ROYAL D'ALEXANDRE

L'INCENDIE DES CŒFFURES

Fig. 21.   "L'Incendie des coeffures" (Photo, Bibliothèque Nationale, Paris).

Fig. 22. "Le perruquier patriote" (Photo, Bibliothèque Nationale, Paris). "The patriotic wigmaker: Yes, my heart goes out to the fatherland. Certainly it has helped me: I shave the clergy, I comb the nobility, and I fit out the Third Estate with wigs."

mous editor, "this title has been adopted by the foreign author as an allusion to the hairstyles of personages in Cochin China who were the official representatives of the three systems."[26]

During the revolutionary period itself the politics of hair were even

26. The "natural hair" represents the legitimate monarchy; the peruke, with its strands liberated from the scalp (*cheveux affranchis*) evokes republicans, who presumably could not produce on their own a truly noble head of hair; the toupee (*faux toupet*), which tries to blend in with what is left of natural hair, is the republican, or constitutional monarchy: it *looks* like the real thing but isn't.

more pronounced, with at least one journalist describing what constituted a patriotic hairstyle (Schama, 525). After Thermidor a popular, though macabre, haircut for women was the startlingly short *coupe à la victime* (Ribeiro, 122).

These last examples link hair to the ultimate subjugation of the condemned man, the *condamné à mort*, whose fate included a ritual humiliation before mounting the scaffold. What was called "faire la toilette du condamné" (grooming the condemned) referred to the obligatory shearing of the victim's hair at the base of the neck.[27] This act was largely symbolic (although hair could interfere with the cleanness of the cut), and it figured prominently in the iconography of the period, especially when the locks to be shorn were of noble length. Thus an engraving of a struggle between a nobleman and a sans-culotte (Fig. 23) has the latter advising the former to watch out for his hair, an oblique reference to what losing it meant. More poignantly, scenes of the final moments of famous personages included shears or hair motifs as foreshadowing of their imminent fate. Engravings of Marie-Antoinette show her cutting her own locks the night before her death (Figs. 24 and 25). A woodblock print of Louis XVI mounting the scaffold portrays one of the executioner's assistants cutting his hair (Fig. 26); another engraving shows the points of the shears ominously approaching the back of his neck (Fig. 27); a third displays the hair and shears on the ground beneath the scaffold (Fig. 28).

During the Revolution, cutting hair became synonymous with cutting necks; Ferdinand Brunot even cites *têtes rasées*, or "shaved heads," as a euphemism during the Terror for the victims of the instrument known as the National Razor. And the fact that the Executioner of Paris was named Sanson (pronounced the same as Sa*m*son, and usually even spelled this way), linked him to another story of hair-cutting, and must have been the source of considerable gallows humor.[28]

Although it might at first seem improbable, this long digression on the history of hair leads back, at least momentarily, to *César Birotteau*, where the same fatal linkage between hair and heads comes up more than once. The first reference occurs in what might be considered the

27. Even before the guillotine the shaving of hair figured as a ritual humiliation of the criminal. On the *toilette du condamné*, see the account in Victor Hugo, *Dernier jour d'un condamné*, in his *Oeuvres complètes*, 2:434–35.

28. In addition, Harrap's *Slang Dictionary* (1983) cites *le grand Coiffeur* ("The Great Barber/Hairstyler") as a slang term for "executioner."

Fig. 23.   "Tiens bien ton bonnet, et toi défend ta queue!" (Photo, Bibliothèque
Nationale, Paris). "Hold on to your hat!—And you, watch out for your hair!" On
the loss of hair as a loss of power, see also Fig. 19: the shears in the queen's right
hand are an allusion to Delilah.

Fig. 24. "Marie-Antoinette dans sa prison" (Photo, Bibliothèque Nationale, Paris). The shears lie on the bed beneath the outstretched hand.

"prehistory" of *César Birotteau*, in a novel that precedes it in the *Comédie humaine*. *Un épisode sous la Terreur* (*An episode during the Terror*, 1830) deals with the plight of the executioner Sanson, who seeks absolution for the regicide he has committed. Significantly, the end of the tale takes place in *La Reine des roses*, the hair-powder shop Birotteau would later purchase from his mentor Ragon.[29] In the later novel, it is Gaudissart who alludes to executions, referring specifically to hair when he recounts his own narrow escape from the guillotine:

> "The uncle of my friend Popinot is a magistrate," Gaudissart said to Finot, "I don't want to bamboozle him; he saved my life. Ah! When one has been in the situation I was in, face to face with the

29. My thanks go to James Winchell for recalling this link between the novels.

Fig. 25.   "La reine de France dans sa dernière prison" (Photo, Bibliothèque
Nationale, Paris). The queen holds the shears on her lap as she reflects on her fate.

LOUIS XVI allant au supplice.

Fig. 26. "Louis XVI allant au supplice" (Photo, Bibliothèque Nationale, Paris).

scaffold, where 'Slice!' and so long hair!" he said while drawing his finger across his throat in imitation of the fatal blade." (*CH*, 6:159)

In the same scene Finot, the author of the prospectus, has changed the name of the tonic from *huile comagène* to *huile céphalique*, that is, from a *hair* oil to a *head* oil; one begins to suspect that the terms are interchangeable.

Of course, *César Birotteau* takes place long after the Revolution, beginning in 1818, and no one's head is on the block—at least, not in the normal sense. There is, however, a kind of death, even an execution, in the works. As César begins to realize how deeply in debt he is, his head swims with so many images of imminent failure that he would like to cut it off: "I wish someone would cut off my head," he says, "I can hardly hold it up" (*CH*, 6:189). More than once he indicates that bankruptcy amounts to a merchant's death (*CH*, 6:220, 271), and each bit of bad news comes like another toll of the financial death knell (*CH*, 6:245). His is no natural demise, however. The embittered du Tillet, who plotted César's downfall from the outset, thirsts for the perfumer's "financial death" (*CH*, 6:279), and he is in a position to obtain it; he sits like a

Fig. 27.   "Le dernier moment de la vie du roi" (Photo, Bibliothèque Nationale, Paris). The shears appear behind the king's left shoulder.

judge, wielding a "power of life or death over him" (*CH*, 6:218). Increasingly the narration casts Birotteau in the terms of a *condamné à mort*, and his bankruptcy in the terms of execution. Adolphe Keller refuses to loan him the necessary funds, and the denial stuns Birotteau "as if the executioner had set the blade on his shoulder to mark the spot" (*CH*, 6:214). Claparon says that Gobseck, the usurer who may be Birotteau's last resort, is as much a banker as the Paris executioner is a doctor, and calls him the "guillotine financière" (*CH*, 6:243). Gigonnet, one of the so-called financiers behind Birotteau's ruin, is referred to as an executioner (*bourreau*) (*CH*, 6:264), and Molineux, named to represent the creditors in the bankruptcy proceedings, is first introduced as a kind of "official executioner" (*exécuteur des hautes oeuvres*) (*CH*, 6:107), who later hopes to brandish bankruptcy law over Birotteau's head like an "axe of justice" (*hache correctionnelle*) (*CH*, 6:280).

Accordingly, César exhibits all the symptoms of the condemned man plunged into despair, so shaky that the night before he files for bank-

Fig. 28.   "Derniers moments de Louis XVI" (Photo, Bibliothèque Nationale, Paris). The shears are highlighted, with the shorn locks, in the triangle of light beneath the scaffold.

ruptcy he cannot keep down his dinner. On the morning that he files, Birotteau is comforted by the abbé Loraux, like a condemned man bolstered by his confessor. When the fatal moment arrives, he tries to brass it out, faltering only when faced with the balance statement he has to sign, when "the poor fellow could not suppress a horrible spasm" (*CH*, 6:261). After this he is officially a *mort civil*.

Caught in the web of a sinister conspiracy, it is hard to see how Birotteau could ever have hoped to escape the fate that awaited him. His hopes, soon abandoned, had rested on a seemingly improbable foundation: "My oil will save us!" he exclaimed to Constance shortly before his collapse.

Of course Birotteau meant that the profits from the sale of the *huile céphalique* will allow him to make ends meet and avoid what is being portrayed as an execution. The tonic designed to preserve people's hair just might allow Birotteau to save his head; it is, after all, a *cephalic* oil. But to do this, to be able to confer not just hair, but the power and life that traditions associate with hair, the *huile céphalique* would have to be magical or divine.

Now, the notion that an oil, when dabbed on the head, might somehow empower an individual is not entirely harebrained. In fact, in France, and since the Middle Ages, just such an act constituted the crucial moment of that quintessential empowerment that is the crowning (*sacre*) of kings. Beginning perhaps with Clovis, kings were anointed with a balm poured from the *sainte ampoule*, a flask (not unlike that found by Popinot for the tonic) borne by angels to the archbishop Rémi. Ever since, the unction of the head constituted *the* essential act of the consecration of kings of France, the act that communicated divine power to the monarch through the pores of his scalp.[30]

César is not entirely incompatible with such kingliness, and his very name conjoins suggestions of regal power and features: the Latin *caesaries*, from which the imperial title originates, refers to a long, full *head of hair*.[31] An unabashed royalist who supplies the king himself with "the only powder he deigns to use" (*CH*, 6:42), and whose shop is only a few steps away from where Louis XVI and Marie-Antoinette were guillotined, he is himself referred to by Pillerault as "the king of men" for his remarkable probity (*CH*, 6:61). Thus recognized as a petit bourgeois "king" of sorts for his own merits, he is also a stand-in for *other* kings, associated now with Louis XVIII, whose emblem he bears as a newly named member of the Légion d'honneur, then with Louis XIV, whose postures he evokes (*CH*, 6:139). Moreover, the remodeling of his apartments, called a *restauration* (and italicized in the text), cannot but call to mind the current political regime—all the more so when Constance complains that the architect is trying to turn their modest living quarters into a Louvre, the royal residence (*CH*, 6:102). However, as César's fate closes in, his kingly traits become more clearly etched: at the same time that he represents a *condamné à mort*, he is depicted as one *condamné* in particular—a royal one. It is not accidental that Birotteau's bankruptcy

30. See Aimé Bonnefin, *Sacre des rois de France*, 91–114. The history of the *Sainte Ampoule* ended with the Revolution, an ardent citizen smashing it on the *parvis* of Rheims in 1793. A few remnants of the balm were reportedly saved, and they were used for the consecration of Charles X in 1830.

31. The imperial title links Birotteau to both the monarchy and the empire; in spite of Birotteau's professed distaste for Napoleon, the novel clearly conflates the Empire and the Restoration (as in *Le Colonel Chabert*).

falls on 15 January, the anniversary of the National Assembly's judgment of Louis XVI in 1793, nor that, in his only precise recording of time of day in the entire novel, Balzac pinpoints César's arrival at the Palais de Justice commercial at "ten-thirty precisely" (*CH*, 6:285), the hour at which the king was executed.

These details put the small story of *César Birotteau* squarely in the context of much larger history, specifically that of the confrontation between the monarchy of the ancien régime and the Revolution. The latter is evoked in the novel by Ferdinand du Tillet. Born in 1793, the bloodiest year of the decade, du Tillet is a true child of the Terror. He is one of the monstrous offspring Balzac sees issuing from the mixture of social species, in this case from the coupling of a "libertine lord" with a "seduced peasant maid" (*CH*, 6:73).[32] Abandoned at birth in the small Norman town of Le Tillet, Ferdinand does his best to conceal his origins, thus transforming his lowly birth into the sign of aristocracy as he appropriates the name of his commune as a surname, adding the particle. Adopted by Birotteau as head clerk, du Tillet responds to his employer's paternal gestures by acts that appear monstrously unnatural: in classic Oedipal style, he attempts to seduce Constance, and vows to annihilate César.[33] Balzac elevates parricide to the level of regicide by describing du Tillet as "a Cromwell intent on cutting off the head of Probity" (*CH*, 6:73). The text also suggests that the assassination includes the now familiar components of ritual cutting of hair. The success of du Tillet's plan depends on separating César from his profit-generating hair tonic, which amounts to a symbolic scalping. It is not for nothing that Balzac describes Birotteau as a *castor poursuivi* (tracked beaver); the beaver is valued for its pelt.

Du Tillet's murderous impulses have their effect. Financially ruined by du Tillet, César enters a squalid existence where every sou is set aside for the payment of his outstanding debts, even though he has no legal obligation to pay them. After two lean years of working at several jobs he finally settles his accounts and is legally rehabilitated by society. Over-

---

32. We have already commented on du Tillet's "monstrous" features, his "figure *chafouine*." The crossing of species is also evoked by the fact that he is called a social "métis," from the Latin *mixtus*, and has "manières mixtes." Clearly he is a crossbreed, which results, the narrator tells us, in the inevitable "défaut de race."

33. Here again is an example of the relativity of the definition of nature. Balzac abhors the monstrosity of du Tillet's acts; but by today's standards, what could be more "natural" than this Oedipal scenario?

whelmed with emotion, César proudly pins on his ribbon of the Légion d'honneur and heads home, only to collapse from physical and emotional exhaustion upon arrival. He expires in Constance's embrace.

Du Tillet, like the Revolution, would seem to get what he wants: César annihilated. However, what the financier had hoped for was César's *commercial* death, and thus the death of his good name; his *physical* death has the opposite effect. The fact that Birotteau works himself into the grave in order to *redeem* himself (and the French expression *se racheter* has both moral and financial overtones), only serves to elevate him to higher honors. Members of the business community are astounded by his commitment to fulfill what is only a moral, and not a legal, obligation; the king himself hears of Birotteau's efforts and encourages them by contributing a small sum to his cause. For du Tillet the whole scheme has backfired, and he finds Birotteau's probity unbearable: "This grand reputation was killing du Tillet" (*CH*, 6:300), especially as the proceeds from the *huile céphalique* allow for the payment of the last outstanding debts, including one to du Tillet himself. The execution du Tillet had planned turns to martyrdom: the hair tonic, much like the balm of the *sainte ampoule*, serves as a guarantee of moral rectitude and divine right, securing a form of spiritual redemption.[34] Financially destitute, Birotteau is far from morally bankrupt. Indeed, he would appear to have achieved the highest moral distinction; the last line of the novel shows Birotteau's ribbon of the Legion of Honor yielding to a more divine decoration: "Jesus orders the Earth to surrender its prey; the holy priest showed Heaven a martyr of commercial probity to be awarded the eternal palm" (*CH*, 6:312).

César's end, already linked to that of Louis XVI, casts both in the light of martyrdom, morality immolated—but not destroyed—by immorality. Present throughout is the suggestion that the Revolution attempted a similar conspiracy, hoping to portray the ancien régime as *morally* bankrupt, yet succeeding only as the architect of its *financial* crises. Both stories suggest that their victims emerge morally enhanced, and both demonstrate exemplary behavior that, if emulated, could leave the door ajar for the return, indeed the *restoration*, of what Balzac sees as an enviable past.

It is tempting at times to read *La Comédie humaine* as an allegory of the French Revolution, but this temptation is best resisted. Balzac *inclines*

---

34. On Birotteau's martyrdom, see Anthony Pugh, "The Ambiguity of *César Birotteau*".

toward allegory, but both *Le Colonel Chabert* and *César Birotteau* challenge the simplification allegory entails. While allegory uses one story to represent another, in Balzac the dynamics are different. For example, Birotteau's petit bourgeois aspirations of retiring to a farm in the provinces do little to cast the king in a flattering light. Instead, it is the concealed story, the history floating just beneath the surface of the novel, that is employed to convey a sense of nobility on Birotteau's efforts.

Rather than allegorize, Balzac uses his evocation of history to demonstrate the inalienable bond between past and present, to show how the present *contains* the past, emulates or distorts it, and is in all cases continuous with it. Novels like *Le Colonel Chabert* and *César Birotteau* are not "really" about the empire or the Revolution; nor are they *romans à clé*, where Chabert figures as a code name for Napoleon, or du Tillet for, say, Robespierre. In fact, as far as Balzac is concerned, this continuity between past and present has nothing literary about it. Rather, it reflects the scientific nature of his enterprise, which strives to show that small events bear the imprint of the larger ones of which they are a part, and that these imprints survive from generation to generation like the traits defining biological species.

More than anything, though, the *Comédie humaine* bears witness to Balzac's fascination with the calamities that disturb the endless repetition of species. That the French Revolution, like Cuvier's natural revolutions, figures as a paradigm for these interruptions, there can be little doubt. Much of Balzac's energy goes into analyzing the monstrous consequences of revolution, and into demonstrating the relentless attempt of the monstrous to disguise itself as the natural.

As we have seen, this attempt focuses on the appropriation of signs, and the Balzacian fascination with imposture accordingly thrives on sartorial codes, physiognomies, and gestures.[35] It is particularly attentive to the usurpation of names: both the Countess Ferraud and du Tillet have maneuvered to lose or distort names that reveal their base origins. Of course, Birotteau is not without his own distortions. As a *parfumeur* his job consists of altering appearances; thus the textual advocate of transparency also embodies figurality. But it is a figurality returned to its docile, classical status, a decorative figurality that *enhances* the truth

35. This attention to detail is especially evident in Balzac's physiologies. See, for example, "Le Notaire" (The Notary), or "La Femme comme il faut" (The Lady of fashion), in Balzac, *Oeuvres diverses*, vol. 3.

without *disguising* it.[36] Such disguises, according to Balzac, never work. His goal is to show that these distortions are never complete, that in the margins of the text or the person, elements of "literalness," of continuity with origins, always come to the surface.

Of course, Balzac's attempt to persuade his readers of the ultimate literalness of signs is itself full of rhetorical posturing. In the margin of the text the authorial hand, busily manipulating an already manipulative narrator, works hard to create the illusion of semiotic integrity. It is here that the text undermines its own authority, as it commits the same sins it condemns. One can only wonder what might have been the reaction of readers when they spotted Balzac taking after his own monsters, fiddling, like the Countess and du Tillet, with his own name and origins, when for the first time in 1830, at the threshold of a text, he signed Honoré *de* Balzac.

36. On the classical perception of rhetorical figures, see Chap. 1.

4 Traveling from the Orient to *Aurélia*: Nerval Looks for the Words

Imagine the diversity, the grandeur, the beauty of a thousand stunning spectacles; the pleasure of seeing nothing but entirely new objects... of observing a somewhat different nature, and of finding oneself in a new world. All this presents to my eyes an inexpressible mixture.
—Rousseau, *La Nouvelle Héloïse*

But how to express this rush of fleeting sensations that I experienced during my walks... ?
—Chateaubriand, *René*

Even if you knew *Les Trembles* as well as I, I would nevertheless have great difficulty making you understand what I found to be so exquisite there.
—Fromentin, *Dominique*

Oh charm of love, who could paint you? No one who has experienced you would ever be able to describe you!
—Constant, *Adolphe*

Poor feebleness of man! With your words, your languages, your sounds, you speak and stammer; you define God, heaven and earth, chemistry and philosophy, and yet you cannot express, with your phrases, all the joy you feel from a naked woman... or a plum pudding!
—Flaubert, *Mémoires d'un fou*

I cannot convey the feeling I had amidst those charming beings, who were dear to me without my even knowing them.
—Nerval, *Aurélia*

Declarations of linguistic inadequacy, such as those above, are the leitmotif of Romantic discourse. Indeed, what is truly *maddening* about the

Romantic hero is that what he fails to articulate is precisely the gravita-
tional center around which his own narrative spins. Just as he reaches
the border of his own radical difference, language falters.

This paradox is part and parcel of the Romantic problem of starting
anew, of addressing issues that had never before been given voice and that
consequently lay beyond the purview of conventional language. Whether
couched in the exoticism and foreignness of the travelogue, in the inti-
macy of personal emotion, in the mysticism of the supernatural or, as in
Nerval's case, in the supreme difference of madness, these issues invariably partook of that extreme "otherness" that fascinated the Romantics,
and for which they struggled to locate words adequate to its representation. In short, the Romantic project consisted largely of attempting to
utter the ineffable.

The Romantic experience of the deficiency of language is yet another
symptom of the changing cultural imagination. While classical linguistics
had characterized language as a potentially complete and transparent
representation of reality (Foucault, *Les mots et les choses*, 112), the
Romantics entertained no such illusions. And with the loss of confidence
in one form of symbolic representation came the need to construct
another, one whose own fictionality would be more resistant to detection. Discourses of "melancholy" (Chambers, *Room for Maneuver*, 107–
8) are thus characterized largely by their desire to create an *alternative*
language, one capable of communicating the extremely personal experience of the Romantic hero.

Yet the methodological problems underlying such an attempt are
legion; in a sense, they foreshadow the difficulties linguistic theory
would later encounter—beyond Frege and into our own day—in accounting for the possibility of any communication at all. For how is one
to present, in language, that which lies beyond language's grasp? Or,
perhaps more troubling, how is one to express *difference* in a discourse based on *convention*, and without betraying the very difference
one desires to communicate? The complaints of the Romantic hero
who suffers absolute solitude will by definition fall on deaf ears; to the
extent that he finds a sympathetic audience, his exclusion and difference wane. The dilemma is illustrated by Alfred de Musset's *Confession
d'un enfant du siècle* (1836), in which the narrator, by announcing his
utter isolation, paradoxically gave voice to the sentiments of an entire
generation.

In the more extreme case of the expression of madness, which will be
important to Nerval, the matter is compounded by the very definition of

the object of study. Michel Foucault has demonstrated that the scientific community of the classical age, and through the early nineteenth century, characterized madness as disorder, privation, and void: the antitheses of rational discourse.[1] The vocabulary of the scientific discourse of the day bears Foucault out:

> Madness, or mental alienation, is a generally chronic and non-febrile cerebral affection, characterized by *disorders* of emotion, reason, and will. (Esquirol, *Des maladies mentales*, 5:5)[2]

> [The word *folie* (madness)] comes from the Latin *follis*, "bellows," "a ball full of air," taken in the sense of *empty head*. (Foville, "Folie," 208)

> Of all human illnesses, surely the saddest and most humiliating is that which *deprives* man of his reason. (Matthey, 65)

> [The madman] presents the portrait of *chaos*. (Esquirol, "Manie," 447)

Thus, while it appears entirely possible to produce a work that talks *about* madness, that is, that describes its external symptoms (Balzac's "Adieu" [1830] and *Louis Lambert* [1832] are cases in point), Nerval was to put himself in the bewildering predicament of trying to write a work that might coherently reproduce the incoherence of the experience itself. Yet madness was seen as being at odds with the very language that might represent it: the disjunctiveness associated with mental illness challenged the notions of syntax and grammar. Although the madman was not entirely divorced from language (for he was regularly perceived to emit a jumble of words), his utterances rang hollow to his "sane" interlocutors. Never mind that the madman himself often seemed to attach a particular *fullness* to his rantings; he was clinically defined by his lack of meaningful

---

1. Foucault asserts that the madman was always defined in terms of negativity; see *Histoire de la folie*, esp. 200, 202, 267–69, 434. That the literary and scientific communities were in touch with each other on this issue has been demonstrated by Ross Chambers ("Récits d'aliénés") and Michel Jeanneret ("La Folie est un rêve").

2. Here and throughout the chapter, all emphasis (save for foreign words) is added, unless otherwise noted.

discourse.[3] Reproducing the voice of madness might presumably be reduced to the mere transcription of the fragmentary ramblings of the deranged, although the words would make no more sense on the printed page than they did in the asylum. The problem for a writer such as Nerval, who drifted back and forth between sanity and its opposite, and who viewed his lapses of reason as so many experiences of plenitude, was that of giving his reader access to madness *in its fullness*.

As it happened, the clinical model of madness as a form of mental chaos or void was undergoing substantial revision in the mid-nineteenth century, around the same time Nerval was working on the problem. In an effort to make their study of insanity more scientifically rigorous, many members of the medical community realized the importance of establishing a reliable definition of the malady, and efforts at definition invariably sought to take as their point of departure a universal constant, an irrefutable sign of either mental health or mental illness.[4] Yet the task was not so simple as it had initially appeared: the "transparent" signs one found in, say, Balzac's *physiologies*, were throwbacks to a sign-system that was radically out of date.[5] Indeed, nothing proved more elusive than a reliable link between madness and its symptoms. The sciences, too, had fallen victim to the collapse of the classical imagination: even this apparently routine attempt to ground psychiatry with a simple definition led to trouble. In 1840 Charles Marc, in a work dealing with the legal distinctions between madness and reason, admitted to considerable confusion between the external signs of the two, commenting on how easy it is to "to mix things up, that is, to attribute to the state of reason that which belongs to the disturbances of this domain, and vice versa" (22). By the early 1870s the search for standards of reason and illness had run into serious trouble:

> Unfortunately, in order to distinguish, by precise definitions, these
> various mental conditions from one another, we must first define

3. At the other extreme from the clinical stance was that of the mystics and many Romantics (Nerval included), who viewed madness as the *vox veritatis*.

4. Foucault writes, "The Psychopathology of the nineteenth century (and perhaps still our own) sets as its center and standard a *homo natura*, or 'normal man,' preceding any experience of illness." In fact, Foucault adds, "this normal man is a fiction" (*Histoire de la folie*, 147).

5. Balzac's descriptions of certain types ("The Notary," "The Lady of Fashion," etc.) presuppose the quasi-phrenological legibility of an individual's characteristics. See Honoré de Balzac, *Oeuvres diverses*, 3:1 194–208.

clearly and absolutely *the normal state of mental faculties, that which one calls reason*; and here we find a first hurdle which no attempts to date have surpassed. (Foville, "Délire," 2)

And scientific scrutiny only further blurred the distinctions psychiatrists sought to reinforce, for attempts at definition continued to fail. By 1872 the project of several decades ended in a pronouncement of defeat by Ambroise Tardieu:

> It would certainly be desirable to be able to assign a specific characteristic to mental alienation and to draw a clear distinction between madness and reason. Many have tried to do so: but without success.... *The pathological sign of madness simply does not exist.* (Tardieu, 59)

Even in certain *scientific* fields, then, signs had become unreliable, and this state of affairs was profoundly troubling. In fact, there emerged during the course of these investigations the unsettling notion that no discernibly *fundamental* difference existed between madness and sanity. How then to account for this otherness that could bear such a resemblance to normalcy? How to handle sanity and insanity without collapsing the distinction altogether? In its search for workable models, psychiatry tested a number of analogies, ranging from dreams to states of intoxication.[6] Another analogy produced around the middle of the century (and resuscitated by Lacan a hundred years later) focused on the concept of language, specifically *foreign* language:[7]

> Moreover, is it altogether sure that we are capable of understanding these patients when they communicate their observations to us? *Don't they rather speak to us in a language which is necessar-*

6. See Jeanneret, "La Folie est un rêve." See also the introductory chapter to the Italian translation of Jeanneret's *La Lettre perdue*, translated as *La scrittura romantica della follia: Il caso Nerval* (Naples, 1984). The first chapter contains a helpful survey of the medical and literary treatment of madness in the nineteenth century. My thanks to Frank Bowman for drawing my attention to this chapter.

7. Why did the linguistic analogy receive relatively little explicit attention at the time? Could it be that while comparisons to dreams and drug-induced states associated madness with what were thought to be abnormal conditions, the comparison to language rendered it uncomfortably close to reason?

ily foreign to us? . . . We see there [in their discourse] . . . only the surface of things; we do not know how to go deeper, to probe the causes, the linkage of mental anomalies. (Moreau de Tours, 33)

Then, in 1853 Alfred Maury was to discuss the internal logic of the madman in startling terms that approached the recognition of a kind of syntax:

> Take the trouble, as I on occasion have done, to put into writing the orderless words, the incoherent utterances of a maniac; compare the words and phrases that he articulates in his delirium, and you will often see the *secret link* which brings together these phrases, so disparate in appearance. Sometimes it is the assonance of the words: the madman associates certain words and, consequently, the ideas that go with them, because these words have the same beginning or ending. Once the words are brought together by an analogy that does not depend on their meaning, the madman will compose sentences with them that will necessarily be incoherent. Sometimes it is the similarity, the sameness of words which nevertheless have different meanings. Thus, for example, the madman will begin his speech with the idea of body [*corps*]. The word *body* [*corps*] evokes, by homonymy, the word *horn* [*cor*], and the statement will end with an idea linked to this last word. (Maury, 405)[8]

These insights, foreshadowing Jakobson's landmark study of the metaphoric and metonymic axes in language disorders (49–74), helped to elevate delirium to the status of a foreign language: the "babbling" of the mad obeyed a different syntax, and one that could be *learned*. Accordingly, the role of the psychiatrist gradually evolved into that of the interpreter.[9] In a radical divergence from earlier practice—and one that

---

8. Emphasis of the words body and horn is Maury's. For more on Alfred Maury, and on the links between the Romantic movement and contemporary scientific enterprises, see Frank Paul Bowman, "Du Romantisme au positivisme."

9. This model has continued, in certain applications, to the present day. Thomas Szasz was to write in *The Myth of Mental Illness*, "I submit that hysteria is nothing more than the 'language of illness,' employed either because another language has not been learned well enough, or because this language happens to be especially useful" (11–12).

would become a cornerstone of Freudian and Lacanian psychoanalysis—clinicians began to lend an ear to the ramblings of their patients.

The scientific acceptance of the meaningfulness of insane discourse may have consecrated a long literary tradition, but it did not in so doing automatically resolve the issue of how to represent this fullness *in its difference*. That is, madness can be viewed as a foreign language, but while such a shift in perspective may provide a definition of the phenomenon, it does not necessarily assist in its interpretation; it does not explain how the "language" of mental illness is to be understood. Indeed, the analogy brings along its own host of problems: the standard method for making foreign discourses accessible to a monoglot culture is translation, and, as the adage drones, *traduttore, traditore*: translation betrays.

The difficulty of translation has been the focal point for recent discussions on the possibility of "vulgarizing" the idiosyncratic idioms of madness. It is unclear to what extent madness can be translated into the dominant discourse without being appropriated, mastered, and domesticated by it. To accept the impossibility of such a project, however, amounts to abandoning madness to its monologic silence. Michel Foucault, in *Histoire de la folie à l'âge classique*, dealt summarily with the problem: he repeated the essentially Romantic gesture of telling his story after affirming its ineffability. After acknowledging in his preface that his task was "doubly impossible" because of what he called a "simple problem of elocution," he essentially bracketed the question in order to proceed to his impossible undertaking.[10]

This error of omission is precisely what Jacques Derrida, in his commentary on *Histoire de la folie*, regards as "the *most insane* part of [Foucault's] project" (*L'Ecriture et la différence*, 56). Derrida asserts that there is no way for Foucault to find a neutral elocutionary space where the discourse of madness might finally speak in its own voice; there is no "metalanguage" so eminently reasonable that it stands outside such oppositions as reason and unreason. Indeed, the very notion of writing a "history" of madness tethers the undertaking to the eminently *rational*

10. For an excellent and more complete outlining of Foucault's program—and of Derrida's critique of Foucault—see Shoshana Felman, *La Folie et la chose littéraire*, esp. 37–55. Foucault's growing realization of his shaky theoretical ground can be seen in the layers of defense provided in the new prefaces for each edition. As if to throw up his hands at the problem, in the last edition before his death Foucault suppressed all previous prefaces in favor of a kind of anti-preface, saying "Let us not look to justify this old book, nor to rewrite it for today" (*Histoire de la folie*, 10).

concept of history (*L'Ecriture et la différence*, 59). It is as if Derrida viewed Foucault's book as an elaborate job of ventriloquism: while Foucault appears to make madness speak, its voice will always be Foucault's own, displaced and muffled. At the very best, madness will be evoked only figuratively: "I mean that the silence of madness is not *spoken*, cannot be spoken in the logos of this book, but presented indirectly, metaphorically" (*L'Ecriture et la différence*, 60).

Here Derrida has hit upon a felicitous image. Although he discusses the metaphorical representation of madness as a *restriction*, metaphor may also provide the only point of access into the hermetic discourse of the insane. To the extent that Enlightenment metaphysics (in fact, perhaps all metaphysics) held figurality to be a kind of dangerous "madness" in language, metaphor might indeed be presumed to have ties to the voice of unreason (see Chapter 1). The trope that *turns* (*trepein*) language away from "proper" usage is a kind of linguistic *deviance* (*deviare*, "to stray from the path"). This link to rhetoric is what leads Shoshana Felman to remove the discussion of madness from historical documents and philosophical or clinical debates, and resituate it within that domain most heavily charged with figurative language: literature (Felman, 15).[11]

However, it is not clear that the invocation of metaphor and the relocation of madness to the realm of fiction do more than postpone addressing the Romantic problem of how to give voice to the ineffable, of how to present the unrepresentable. While it is true that the Romantic narrative generally teems with explicit figures (one need only think of the first paragraphs of the *Confession d'un enfant du siècle*), the reader's perception of otherness remains irremediably indirect. Metaphor does not resolve the problems inherent to the translation of difference, for it is merely *another form* of translation, often glibly construed as the translation of the unknown into the known. Indeed, it is not insignificant that the words are etymologically identical, *translatio* and *metapherein* both evoking a "carrying across"; moreover, in Latin the terms *translatio* and *metaphora* were partially interchangeable, the former denoting both translation *and* metaphor. If the language of modernity could provide any direct experience and understanding of otherness, it would only be to the extent that it can move beyond the reductive translation of conventional metaphor.

The question of how to make the sphinx of otherness talk has re-

11. For further discussion along the same lines as Felman, see Jeanneret, *La Lettre perdue*, 10–11.

mained, then, infuriatingly unresolved. However, between the tendency of the early Romantics to beg the question and that of modern ironists to regard it as an insoluble riddle, one would hope to find some middle ground. This ground is occupied by a figure situated on the cusp of Romanticism and irony: Gérard de Nerval. If anyone could translate the untranslatable, it was he; indeed, Jean Richer was to write of *Aurélia* in 1947 that, "the work . . . makes an essentially incommunicable experience magically accessible" (Richer, ix). Of course, "magic" is the realm of illusion, of smoke and mirrors. Nerval will never step outside the irremediable mediation of language. What is of interest here, however, is how he creates the illusion of doing so, how the strategies of his particular act of fiction create the impression that one has moved *past* translation and *into* the direct experience of otherness.

Nerval was sensitive to the limitations inherent in translation even before he undertook to introduce his readers to the world of delirium in which he often sojourned. Entering the literary scene in 1828 with a new rendering of *Faust*, he prefaced his version of the epic with comments pertaining to the ultimate *impossibility* of translation: "Here is a third translation of *Faust*; and what is certain is that none of the three can say, '*Faust* is translated!' It is not that I wish to cast any aspersions on the work of my predecessors, the better to conceal the weaknesses of my own, but rather that I consider a satisfactory translation of this stunning work to be impossible" (preface to *Faust*, 1).

"Impossible" presumably because of the idiosyncrasies of language: German is not simply a code of French, and its idioms are idiomatic precisely to the extent that they can be said to resist translation. What is "lost" in translation is the "German-ness" of the original; or, if not lost, it is at least "exchanged" (in an essentially metaphoric transaction) for French nonequivalents.[12]

The fact that Nerval knew translation to be irremediably flawed did not keep him from pursuing his interest in it, nor from enlarging its scope in his own work. He did not content himself with the translation of language per se (although he did continue with it, translating Heine, for example, through the 1840s); he was even to expand his role as interpreter into the various domains of culture, history, society, and, of course, mental states. In a sense, translation could be considered the

---

12. Nor is French a code for English: my (English) translation of Nerval's (French) assertions about the untranslatability of the (German) original would seem to compound the problem. On this methodological quandary, see Chapter 1.

overarching image of his work. From the *Chansons et légendes du Valois* (1854) to *Les Illuminés* (1852), from the *Voyage en Orient* (1848–51) to *Aurélia* (1855), Nerval sought to communicate to his readers special knowledge to which he alone was privy.

Certainly, the same could to some extent be said of every author, for narrators always mediate between reader and story. Nerval, however, does not introduce the reader to an otherness he has viewed from the outside, but to an intimate circle of which he is an initiate. He can thus mediate in good faith precisely because of the privileged status of the translator, who straddles the boundary between sameness and difference. Nerval can appreciate the difficulties of translation because he speaks *both* German *and* French (*Faust*), because he is in some sense a product of *both* the eighteenth *and* the nineteenth centuries (*Les Illuminés*),[13] because he is *both* pagan *and* Christian ("Isis"),[14] because he has been *both* sane *and* mad (*Aurélia*).

The difference between inside and outside perspectives might best be illustrated in the case of the Romantic travelogue, and one might usefully compare Chateaubriand's *Itinéraire de Paris à Jérusalem* (1811) to Nerval's *Voyage en Orient* (*Trip to the Orient*, 1851 [definitive edition]). Chateaubriand allegedly undertakes his journey in order to *confirm* preconceived ideas: "I had determined the structure of *Les Martyrs*. Most of the volumes of this book had already been sketched out; I thought I should not put the finishing touches on them before seeing the country where my story takes place" (5, 109). Thus Chateaubriand's travels are marked by the desire to see what he already knows, especially structures or landscapes referred to in books he has read—or previously written. Traveling with an escort and maintaining the profile of a *grand seigneur*,[15] he represents a pocket of Frenchness while abroad. As such, he is sensitized primarily to that with which he can identify:

> I enjoyed happening upon the vestiges of French honor, beginning
> with my first steps in the true fatherland of glory and in the country

13. Nerval comments repeatedly on his education in eighteenth-century literature through his uncle, as well as on his uncle's peculiar library. His affinity for the earlier century is especially clear in the similarities evident between Rétif de la Bretonne and Nerval in "M. Nicolas," in *Les Illuminés*.

14. "Isis" (1845) is essentially a story of the transformation, or translation, of pagan images into Christian ones, specifically of Isis into the Virgin Mary.

15. See Claude Pichois' *Notice* to the *Voyage en Orient*, in Gérard de Nerval, *Oeuvres complètes*, 2:1377.

of a people which had recognized true merit. But where does one not find these vestiges! In Constantinople, in Rhodes, in Syria, in Egypt, in Carthage; everywhere I landed I was shown the French camp, the French tower, the French castle; the Arab showed me the tombs of our soldiers under the sycamores of Cairo, as the Seminole [showed me those] under the poplars of Florida. (5:125)[16]

Chateaubriand is also supremely untroubled by the question of language: his narrative incorporates almost no record of local tongues (foreign language in the *Itinéraire* consists principally of Italian and Latin, which are used only ornamentally), and Chateaubriand proceeds almost as if the *drogman*, or translator, were neither present nor necessary.

Nerval, on the other hand, takes a different tack. For one thing, he dispenses with the monumental descriptions that had become a convention of the genre. Moreover, attempting to shed his identity as a Frenchman, he moves increasingly throughout the narrative toward a direct experience of the otherness of Middle Eastern life. In the lingo of modern anthropologists, he takes a step toward "going native." He thus rejects the French hotels in favor of a home in a comfortable Arab neighborhood of Cairo, conforms to local custom by adding a woman slave to his household, and much later will successfully disguise himself as a Persian in order to take up quarters in Istanbul during Ramadan[17]. Yet in spite of his assimilation, language remains a barrier. Unlike Chateaubriand's *Itinéraire*, the *Voyage* presents translation, incarnated in the form of the narrator's *drogman*, as *the* central problem of Nerval's experience of otherness, and it is one Nerval elaborates thematically. Relying at first on international *bonhomie*, the narrator is soon alerted to the dangers of translation by Youssef, a casual acquaintance:

> "I heard," he told me, "that they made you buy a slave; I'm quite upset about it."

---

16. One is reminded of Levi-Strauss' travelers who, when brought to New York, judge it according to European cities, the terms of their own existence (*Tristes tropiques*, 85). The reverse side of this experience is Flaubert, who, years later, complains that he cannot escape France in the Orient. The passage is commented on in Richard Terdiman's *Discourse/Counter-Discourse* (240–41). The cultural collision between the East and the West resulted in, one might say, a serious occident.

17. *Oeuvres complétes*, 2:637. All further reference to the *Voyage en Orient* will be to this edition, hereafter cited as *OC*.

"Why is that?"

"Because they have certainly cheated or robbed you: the *drogmans* are always in cahoots with the slave trader. . . . Abdallah will have received at least one purse for himself." (*OC*, 2:349)

The narrator's realization that his interpreter—indeed, that translation as a whole—is unreliable and inadequate, leads him to dismiss Abdallah, and to take the only course of action left open. Immediately following the interpreter's departure comes the chapter, "First Lessons in Arabic" (*OC*, 2:353), and the text is hereafter liberally sprinkled with transcriptions of words from a variety of tongues, principally Arabic and Turkish. In addition to producing the first occurrence in French literature of such words as *baklava* (*OC*, 2:638), the narrator's entrance into oriental languages (much more successful, in fact, than Nerval's own) signals an important shift in perspective. Unwilling to remain at the mercy of his *drogman*, he works to *replace* him, to move himself into the privileged position of translator that Nerval's narrators customarily occupy. Although he occasionally has recourse to such intermediaries as Mme Bonhomme and other displaced Europeans, the narrator eventually achieves a degree of self-sufficiency. It is thanks to this straddling of languages and cultures that he is able, during the *fête du Ramadan* to steal into Istanbul, where "no Christian has the right to reside" (*OC*, 2:636). Here, in the longest and last narration of the book, he himself will fulfill for the reader the role of *drogman*, providing a translation of the legend of Adoniram.

In the *Voyage en Orient* Nerval took steps to resolve the problem of how to "get at" foreignness, and his solution consisted of dismissing mediation, of confronting otherness directly, and of learning its logic. However, he did not address the issue of how to communicate this foreignness directly to his reader. Just as the narrator of the *Voyage* is originally at the mercy of his *drogman*, so the reader finds himself entirely dependent on the mediation of the narrative voice. Of course, Nerval's accounts and translations are no less transparent than those of the scheming Abdallah. The interpreter lost his job for failing to translate neutrally, that is, for fabricating, for entering into *fiction*. Nerval, whose true itinerary strayed significantly from that of his narrative, and whose "legend" of Adoniram was less translated than fabricated, was guilty of as much.

Nevertheless, the *Voyage en Orient* can be seen as an essential step toward the achievement of Nerval's other objective: the presentation of the ultimate otherness of madness *in its fullness*.[18] The *Voyage* suggests that although translation betrays, the translator himself enjoys unmediated interaction with foreignness, a foreignness he will nevertheless be unable to render. Introducing one's readers to a direct experience of otherness would entail allowing *them* to accede to the position of translator. They must, in a sense, repeat the narrator's usurpation of the place of Abdallah; this time, however, the reader would supplant the narrator himself. It is for this reason that, in *Aurélia*, when he tries to introduce readers to the extreme otherness of madness, Nerval surrenders the model of translation for that of language acquisition. To understand madness, the reader needs to learn how to speak it.

It is not insignificant that a similar approach to the study of madness was being advocated in the clinic. As we saw earlier, figures such as Moreau de Tours and Maury had adopted a model of mental illness that likened it to foreign language. Yet it remained unclear what the clinical applications of this model might be.

Surprisingly, what might be considered an unrecognized breakthrough in this respect came from the practice of a rather retrograde clinician, François Leuret. In 1846 Leuret published a slender manual for practicing psychiatrists, entitled *Des indications à suivre dans le traitement moral de la folie*. Although a student of Esquirol, Leuret's methods tended toward those of pre-Pinelian psychiatry, relying heavily on intimidation and on such characteristically eighteenth-century therapies as the *bain de surprise*. What is the most revealing in the series of cases outlined in *Des indications à suivre* is the occasional account of Leuret's irascibility. One such account occurs in the report on a certain Mme Louise, who was plagued and terrified by visions of communion hosts. When the young woman failed to respond to therapy, Leuret succumbed to a petty desire to vent his frustration on his patient. But how could he obtain satisfaction from a person who was not responsive to his professional terrorism? In a moment of inspired malice, Leuret called for a box

18. For Nerval, the otherness of the Orient was in some ways analogous to that of madness. Thus, in *Aurélia*, when the narrator heads into delirium, he proclaims to a friend that he is headed "for the Orient." For other links between the *Voyage en Orient* and *Aurélia*, see Jeanneret, "Sur le *Voyage en Orient* de Nerval."

of sealing wax, the white disks of which resemble the host; the doctor then threatened to scatter them about the room, much to Mme Louise's horror (Leuret, 15–32).[19]

Leuret illustrated, albeit unwittingly, a radical and enlightening departure from standard clinical practice. Despairing of his chances for making his patient adopt the language of "reason," he entered into the alienated discourse of Mme Louise. Linking "getting mad" to "going mad," Leuret interacted and communicated with his patient *on her own terms*. Indeed, he seemed to have learned her logic so well that an outsider happening upon the scene of a man hurling wafer-shaped pieces of wax at a cowering victim might well have been hard-pressed to determine which figure represented the cause of science and which the face of insanity.

Nerval's bouts with mental illness were perfectly contemporaneous with Leuret's fiascoes and with the development of the linguistic model of madness, a model increasingly sanctioned by the medical community, and with which Nerval's own views can be shown to be entirely consonant.

His strategies for communicating otherness did not, then, form in a vacuum. In the same year that Maury's article on the "secret links" of delirious discourse appeared in the *Annales Médico-psychologiques* (1853), Nerval began serious work on *Aurélia* (published in *La Revue de Paris* in the beginning of 1855, the second part appearing shortly after the author took his own life). The narrator of this work—closely associated with Nerval himself—undertakes to describe his encounters with madness. He also relates what is often understood as his "cure": at the end of the novel the main character emerges from the sanitarium with a newfound control over language. As the character becomes the narrator of his own story, a series of oppositions pitting narrator against hero, sanity against madness, and past against present, seem to end in resolution.

However, Nerval explicitly rejects the notion that *Aurélia* is the story of a cure, resisting from the outset the analogy of illness: "I am going to try ... to transcribe the impressions of a long illness which took place entirely within the mysteries of my mind; and I do not know why I use

19. It is interesting to note that Nerval's own doctor, Esprit-Sylvestre Blanche, had earlier decried Leuret's methods, which touted "the desirable effects of *intimidation* in the treatment of madness" (Blanche, 5–6). On Nerval's relationship with his doctors, especially Blanche and his son, see Peter Dayan, *Nerval*.

the term illness, for never, as far as I am concerned, have I felt myself to be in better health" (*O*, 1:359).[20]

Moreover, the final lines of the novella assert the positive nature of the narrator's experiences: "Nevertheless, I am happy for the beliefs I have acquired, and I compare this series of trials that I have undergone to what the Ancients saw in a descent into Hell" (*O*, 1:414).

Aurélia thus figures as a kind of *roman d'éducation*, although not in the traditional sense, for it is not the protagonist who is in need of schooling. He already possesses the special knowledge he hopes to relate; the implied "student" of the educational narrative is none other than the reader.

Nerval then undertakes, in the manner of Alfred Maury, to illustrate the "secret links," the hidden logic of madness. He explicitly strives to "transcribe" the impressions of his so-called illness (*O*, 1:359). The word "transcribe" would seem to suggest that Nerval intends to record elements of his experience without resorting to mediation. Yet it quickly becomes apparent that this record—at least at the outset—will come with a commentary. The narrator positions himself as the *translator* of the hieroglyphic language of dream and madness. That some form of translation or interpretation is needed becomes evident in the inaugural line: "Le Rêve est une seconde vie" (Dreams are a second life). Not only does this assertion suggest a mysterious articulation between sleeping and waking states, but the capitalization of "Rêve," as Ross Chambers has shown, elevates dream to the level of allegory, one that virtually begs for interpretation ("Récits d'aliénés," 78–79).

The narrator bolsters the view of himself as interpreter, *drogman* if you will, by allusions to earlier texts that serve as models for his own enterprise: Virgil's *Aeneid,* Swedenborg's *Memorabilia,* Apuleius's *Golden Ass,* and Dante's *Divine Comedy* and *Vita nuova.* Significantly, all these texts are linked to problems of interpretation: each written in a language foreign to Nerval and each depicting a world so laden with mysterious analogies that they require the assistance of a guide or commentator.

Just as the poet of the *Vita nuova* explains the structures and images of his verse, so Nerval's narrator sets about interpreting "the invisible world" (*O*, 1:359), "the world of illusion in which I sojourned for some

20. At the time of this writing, the volume containing *Aurélia* in the new Pichois edition had not yet appeared. All citations from *Aurélia* thus refer to the Béguin and Richer edition (*Oeuvres*, [Paris: Gallimard, 1974]); hereafter cited as *O*.

while" (*O*, 1:414). Thus when he crosses paths with Aurélia in another city, the narrator links her greeting to a divine pardon that transforms his "profane" love, inscribing it with a new sign:

> How was I to interpret this action and the deep, sad gaze which she added to her greeting? I thought I saw in it the pardon of the past; the divine accent of pity made those simple words she spoke to me inexpressibly dear, as if something religious were blending with the sweetness of a love heretofore profane, and *imprinting* upon it *the character* of eternity. (*O*, 1:361)

The narrator intervenes regularly as a commentator to assist us (insofar as he is able) in our reading, particularly in the deciphering of dreams. "One perceives fairly easily in the father and mother the analogy of the electric forces of nature," he interprets after the dream of chapter 4, "but how can one see the individual centers emanating from them, from which they emanate, as a collective animistic *figure*?" (*O*, 1:369, emphasis in original). Or, after a particularly perplexing dream: "What did it mean? I did not know until later. Aurélia was dead" (*O*, 1:374).

These visions can be understood by the reader precisely because of the narrator's position as polyglot, fluent in the various discourses of reason and madness. The linguistic analogy is one he himself invokes: in his attempt to synthesize a history of the world, he tries to incorporate "a thousand figures accompanied by stories, verses, and inscriptions in all known languages" (*O*, 1:375). Similarly, in his dreams he recognizes meaning in what appears to be the mere "confused chattering" of birds (*O*, 1:379), and seems even to divine meaning: "Such were the words, more or less, that were either spoken to me, or whose meaning I thought I had grasped" (*O*, 1:383).

Such passages clearly partake of the mode of translation; yet the function of translation in *Aurélia* is not that of rendering madness totally transparent, of forcing it to imitate the language of reason. In order not to betray the essential difference of the discourse of madness, Nerval retains elements of his dreams in his prose, principally those indicating discontinuity and juxtaposition. Part 1 is thus marked by a certain number of ellipses and parataxes (Chambers "Récits d'aliénés," 79), as well as by a repeated expression of the untranslatability of certain ideas:

> The divine accent of pity made her words ... *inexpressibly* dear. (*O*, 1:361)

> While walking I sang a mysterious hymn . . . which filled me with an *ineffable* joy. (*O*, 1:363)

> *I cannot convey* the feeling I had amidst those charming beings. (*O*, 1:371)

> *I do not know how to explain* that, to my mind, earthly events could coincide with the those of the supernatural world. (*O*, 1:380)

The problem of the ineffable situates Nerval squarely within the parameters of Romantic discourse, a discourse scarred by the collapse of what we have called the classical imagination. The question then becomes how, given the newfound indeterminacy and mutability of language, the Romantic is ever to express meaning. Certainly not by means of conventional discourse, whose steady disintegration *Aurélia* chronicles. Indeed, at the final stage of this disintegration, and as if to punctuate it, the narrator refers to his library as nothing more than "the Tower of Babel in two hundred volumes" (*O*, 1:406).

Tellingly, the narrator's conclusion that language has failed him coincides with the erruption of conflict within his dream world, and this conflict results in the abandoning of translation. The crisis occurs at the end of part 1, when the parallel worlds between which Nerval's narrator divides his time suddenly turn incompatible. The inability of Nerval's language to translate, to transparently *figure* his supernatural experience, manifests itself in the narrator's incompatibility with the figure who parallels his own existence: his double. "*The other* is my enemy," he says of his mystical brother (*O*, 1:381). Later, "I know he has already struck me with his weapons, but I await him without fear, and I know the sign which is to vanquish him" (*O*, 1:384).

The clash signals the disintegration of parallelism between what the narrator calls the "internal" and "external" worlds: "What had I done? I had upset the harmony of the magic universe which gave my soul the assurance of immortal existence" (*O*, 1:385). As his position disintegrates, the narrator becomes less and less capable of expressing the meanings of his other world, a difference that will necessarily elude conventional discourse. The very language that was to have been the vehicle of translation reveals itself to be fundamentally flawed: "The magical alphabet, the mysterious hieroglyph come to us incomplete and distorted either by time, or by those who have an interest in our ignorance" (*O*, 1:387). To repair this imperfection, the narrator hopes to "recover the lost letter [*la lettre perdue*] or the erased sign" (*O*, 1:387), thus restoring the ability of language to render the meaning of his altered states. However, his hopes are not realized: "The dream became confused" (*O*, 1:392), and the only sense the narrator vaguely deciphers consists of a reprimand: "All this was done in order to teach you the secret of life, and you have not understood. Religions and fables, saints and poets all came together to explain the fatal enigma, *and you interpreted wrong*" (*O*, 1:392).

The ability of language to convey meaning, to translate adequately, appears to have collapsed. In this respect, Nerval's plight is not unrelated to Balzac's; both are troubled by upheavals in the world of signs. Unlike the novelist, however, Nerval does not deny the seriousness of the rupture between signs and meanings, nor does he cling, as did Balzac, to the shreds of a language that seemed to have lost its fullness. Nerval's disillusionment with language is more profound than Balzac's. While his predecessor managed to shore up semiotic integrity, as we saw in Chapter 3, Nerval finds himself in a desperate situation: the disintegration of sign systems, or at least of Nerval's ability to manipulate them, undermines all his attempts at symbolic resolution. Indeed, Nerval's plight is that he now needs to resolve the problem (at least symbolically) of the inadequacy of symbolic resolutions. He will do so by a powerful act of fiction. Unable to abide the insanity of a language cut adrift from meaning, he works in the mode of reconstruction, forging a new discourse. This new discourse will always be full for Nerval, but only because it will be full *of* Nerval. For the insane irony of conventional language Nerval will substitute the personal idiolect of madness. In so doing, he relies implicitly on the current medical analogies, which (as we have seen) validated the legitimacy of such "personal" languages.[21]

Giving himself over to *one* language, that of plenitude, Nerval sidesteps the problems of mediating between two discourses, of translating. Accordingly, interpretation ceases within the text. In part 2 of *Aurélia*, the narrative commentary, which had previously translated the dream discourse, all but disappears. These chapters are marked by many discursive gaps; interjections, ruptures, or changes of narrative perspective are framed merely by blank lines, or by ellipses. Distinctions regularly made in part 1 between past and present, between narrator and protagonist,

---

21. Ross Chambers has shown how even before this shift in the text the narrator has recruited a sympathetic reader by grafting the "insane" discourse on other medical analogies, especially that of the dream (*Room for Maneuver*, 131–32).

often vanish. Both thematically and graphically the language of "sanity" begins to falter: the narrator loses his record of the location of Aurélia's tomb; the letters to her that he announces are missing; words themselves begin to disintegrate, "Aurélia" turning into the letter "A" followed by three asterisks, and finally shrinking merely to the three asterisks. With the effacement of the narrator and the predominance of a new semantics, the textual discourse begins to resemble the source language more than the target language, and the reader must fend for himself.

What has happened is that the novella has tried to move from the interpretation of madness to its presentation, from the *translation* of madness to its *transcription*. The narrative commentary of part 1, having served as a primer to the otherness of madness, now fades, forcing the reader to confront this otherness without mediation; that is, to accede to the role of translator himself, and to read the secret links. Thus the fading of Aurélia's name might be read as a representation obeying a different logic: associated earlier with the narrator's *star* of destiny, she is now reduced to asterisks, which, as the Greek root *aster* implies, are but "little *stars*."

That one must read *Aurélia* in such a "perverse" fashion (not just rhetorically, but hieroglyphically) is the crux of the matter. It is in the dicey indeterminacy of rhetoric that Nerval formulates a grammar, whose "secret links" can only occasionally be gleaned.[22] The reader's instruction in this new language has two components: the first part of the novella constitutes a sort of language primer, one that outlines the rudiments of the hero's "insane" grammar; next, the near disappearance of the narrator in part 2 of *Aurélia* corresponds to the narrative plan of the *Voyage en Orient*. That is to say, the *drogman*—here the narrator himself—has been dismissed. After the brief lesson of part 1, the reader, able to straddle discourses, is left to step into the role of translator.

The fact that one is able to decipher any of part 2 at all is a credit to the apprenticeship given earlier; indeed, generations of critics have tossed up their hands at the difficulty of the end of *Aurélia*.[23] But part 1

22. Evidence that one can indeed learn aspects of Nerval's language can be seen in Christopher Prendergast's reading of "Sylvie" (*The Order of Mimesis*, 148–79).

23. Two readings have helped immensely in penetrating this part of the text. See Jean Richer, *Gérard de Nerval et les doctrines ésotériques*, esp. the discussion of tarot and numerology. Frank Paul Bowman fills in many of the gaps and offers a brilliant reading of the historical allusions in the *Mémorables* (*French Romanticism*, 167–81).

has shown that the language of Nerval's madness is to be read allegorically, or iconographically, or even hieroglyphically. Thus the narrator's aimless peregrinations through Paris, related in chapter 4 of part 2 (*O*, 1:396–98), might be construed as corresponding to the disorder of his mind, as well as to the wandering of various signifiers: Notre-Dame changes into Notre-Dame de Lorette and Notre-Dame-des-Victoires; the candles in the church reappear in the night sky; the inscription "Allah! Mohamed! Ali!" is echoed in the choral repetition "Christe! Christe! Christe!"; and the priest ("l'abbé Dubois") becomes the psychiatrist ("they took me to the Dubois clinic [*la maison Dubois*]"). Lunacy itself is inscribed in the narrator's vision of the "moons streaming across the sky," and the textual divagations resemble the narrator's sense that "the earth was drifting in the firmament like a dismasted vessel."

That a concentrated allegorical logic is also at work in this passage is evidenced by the narrator's self-destructive impulse when he reaches the Place de la Concorde: "Having arrived at the place de la Concorde, my thoughts turned to suicide." The Concorde can be established as the intersection—or the point of concordance—of various levels of reading. It is significant not only because of its intertextuality (the image of the obelisk evoking one of René's images from a similar peregrination: "Sometimes a tall column appeared standing alone in a desert, just as a great thought rises . . . in a ravaged soul" [Chateaubriand, *Oeuvres romanesques*, 1:122]), but also because the square is, from the time of the Revolution, associated with death. (During the Revolution the place de la Concorde had been renamed the place de la Révolution, and was the principal site for public executions.) Furthermore, the place de la Concorde marks the beginning of the Champs-Elysées (the narrator's original destination), the other end of which is defined, in Parisian toponymy, by the place de l'Etoile. The mention of the Champs-Elysées, the "Elysian Fields," recalls the Virgilian descent into hell evoked at the beginning of the text, as well as the descent of Orpheus, referred to in the epigraph of part 2. Both of these classical allusions serve as metaphors for Nerval's descent into madness: he later remarks that "I compare this series of trials . . . to what the Ancients saw in a descent into Hell" (*O*, 1:414). For the Ancients such descents were positive encounters (leading to knowledge for Aeneas and to a glimpse of Eurydice for Orpheus), and Nerval clearly views such a descent as a possibility to recover what has been lost. So, in the passage in question, the fact that the Champs-Elysées should lead to l'Etoile suggests that the narrator sees a descent into the Elysian Fields of the dead—presumably achieved through suicide—as the only possibility of reaching l'Etoile, that little star, the asterisk that Aurélia has become.

One finds similar complexity in the hero's encounter with "Saturnin," the fellow-patient in the asylum (*O*, 1:407–8). The apparently arbitrarily selected name ("I don't know why it occurred to me that his name was Saturnin" [*O*, 1:408]), is a near anagram of the adjective the narrator has used to describe him: taciturn. On another register, the resonance "Saturn" calls to mind the mythological Golden Age, the *aureas aetas*, an original utopia ruled by Saturn, and one in which Astraea, the "Star-maiden" (later to be associated with the constellation Virgo, thus joining the Nervalian fascinations of the star and the Virgin) watched over mankind. Saturnin is thus linked to Aurélia, "the golden one,"[24] and Nerval continues with the references to a mythological scene when he calls his companion "indefinable" and compares him to a sphinx. The notion of the sphinx implicitly ties Saturnin to the "fatal enigma" (*O*, 1:392) used to describe the dream discourse. Moreover, the narrator's coaxing of Saturnin into speech corresponds to the process of language acquisition practiced upon the taciturn reader of *Aurélia*; Saturnin is in fact emblematic of a reader confronted with a discourse he must learn (or relearn) in order to speak (Chambers, *Maneuver*, 131–40). Indeed, he represents everything to which the narrator has tried to give voice: dreams, images, hallucinations, and Aurélia herself.

The reader who begins to understand this textual logic, to "acquire" this language, can begin to appreciate the otherness and fullness of Nerval's alternative discourse. Indeed, the sense of resolution pervading the end of the story, in contrast to the frustration so prevalent earlier, seems to derive from a sense that communication has finally been achieved *without* the distortions of translation.

Yet, for all of its ingenuity, Nerval's shift from a model of translation to one of language acquisition is not altogether unproblematic.[25] Although the fading of the narrator serves to allow the reader into the position of translator, this effacement can never be complete. Furthermore, the success of *Aurélia* in representing Nerval's delusions depends on the validity of the linguistic analogy of madness, which is itself perhaps only one

---

24. For further discussion of the importance of the Golden Age in *Aurélia*, see Françoise Gaillard, "Aurélia ou la question du nom," 240, 245.

25. The majority of readings have viewed *Aurélia* as a clinical "success" story (see Jeanneret's influential reading in *La Lettre perdue*, 170); some have sensed the incompleteness of the adventure of *Aurélia* (see esp. Lynne Huffer, 39–50).

more translating metaphor by which a discourse of otherness is appropriated into a dominant vocabulary. Moreover, even if the new language Nerval proposes is in some sense "hieroglyphic"—and therefore akin to the supposedly pictorial, figurative origin attributed to language by eighteenth-century linguistics (see Chapter 1)—Nerval can never quite escape language completely. He may, at best, attenuate its effects. However, the *reduction* of distortion does not imply its *elimination*, and Nerval cannot transcend the basic properties of a language—"insane" or otherwise—that will necessarily distort experience while structuring it in terms of linguistic logic. Avoiding translation removes only one of the layers of mediation in language.

Nerval is not oblivious to these problems. Although it seems clear that for him concerns of language and reason overlap considerably, and that his particular world is indeed susceptible to the linguistic analogy of madness, he nevertheless suggests that he has grasped incompletely the link between "the internal and external worlds" (*O*, 1:413). The internal world remains just beyond his reach.[26] This is not because something has been lost *in* translation, an activity the narrator has avoided, but because something was lost *before* translation, even before language: Aurélia herself. This loss that exists outside of language (indeed, that Nerval's language, in all its contortions, attempts to fill), remains irremediably beyond the experience of the reader. The narrator's series of losses, of Aurélia once and even "a second time" (*O*, 1:385), of her correspondence, of the very tomb that marks her absence, makes of Aurélia a version of that *lettre perdue,* that if found, would provide fullness. Indeed, in her disintegration from a proper noun to "A***" and finally "***," Aurélia becomes the *lettre qui se perd*. Vanishing even as a letter, Aurélia thus eludes language, and it is this loss that Nerval will never be able to render.

The ambivalence of the conclusion of *Aurélia*, where the narrator oscillates between a fondness for and the abandonment of his delirium, and where the narrative straddles its end and its beginning, evokes the equivocation of the reader. Having acceded to the position of translator, the reader is able to enter into another language; in so doing, however, he glimpses the inadequacy of language (and fiction) as a whole, as it never does more than camouflage in various vocabularies the losses it cannot fill.

26. "I thought I understood that there existed between the internal and external worlds a link; that inattention or mental disturbances distorted only the superficial bonds between them" (1:413).

Nerval's strategy of reconstruction, of attempting to lay a foundation for a new language, one that might recover the integrity of a mythical primitive tongue, leads to the most dreadful of discoveries. He struggles to escape the opposition pitting the literal against the figurative, and hopes to invent a form of representation that is neither one nor the other. Yet that way lies madness, and far from providing an oasis of meaningfulness in an otherwise desolate world, madness reveals itself to be the abyss of irony Nerval had sought to avoid. The meaningfulness madness has promised is always *almost*; it is always an illusion concealing an absence, always a disappointment. Meaning, it turns out, rather than being that which representation represents, resides in representation itself. When Nerval lifts the veils of representation in order to *see* truth without mediation, *nothing is there*. In the end, madness reveals the endless *peregrination* of meaning within representation, an aimlessness that for Nerval was cause for despair.

5 The Esthetic Mask: Irony and Allegory in Baudelaire's *Spleen de Paris*

In Chapter 2 we saw how Sade's narrative confronted the structures of the ancien régime, undermining their legitimacy by exposing them as fictions. The results were predictable. Governments have a vested interest in diverting attention from the fictionality of their authority, and in eighteenth- and nineteenth-century France officials safeguarded governmental power by employing a time-honored practice: censorship. Censorship might thus be defined as the operation by which one fiction is protected from others. Contestatory voices are silenced, defused, or otherwise disabled.

The practice leads to a compelling question: if the dominant culture has the means to subdue competing discourses, how could such discourses ever survive? Of course, even during the heyday of censorship in France, many did survive. During the nineteenth century no one could attack every piece of hack oppositional journalism, or prosecute the author of every dirty drinking song. There is, in short, an economy of censorship: when the energy required to suppress a text is judged to exceed the energy lost by allowing it, the authorities let it slide.

The strategies for avoiding censorship, if this is all one wants, are not complicated: either one moderates one's challenge so as not to arouse the interest of the authorities (what we call "self-censorship"), or one encodes one's attack, and the text becomes a kind of "secret message" decipherable only by those trained in the code. However, neither strategy is particularly effective at maintaining the contestatory nature of the work. In the first case, the challenge remains public, but neutralized; in the second, it retains its virulence, yet reaches only a private audience, preaching, as it were, to the converted. The problem is, how does one expose the fictionality of authority without exposing oneself to censorship (see Wing, 6)? How can one challenge legitimacy in a way that is neither altogether private nor entirely sterile?

These questions were to take on special urgency during the Second Empire, a regime whose claim to legitimacy was at best fragile.[1] Oscillating between republican ideals and reactionary bullying, Louis Napoleon began by extolling the virtues of a free press, only to resort to censorship measures of surprising severity when the press began biting the hand that had caressed it. Eighteen fifty-seven appeared as a year of key importance in the censorship debate: first Flaubert came to trial for publishing *Madame Bovary* in *La Revue de Paris*; then, six months later, public scrutiny was focused on Charles Baudelaire.

True, Baudelaire had never been one to cater to middle-class sensibilities. Indeed, dating from such early endeavors as the *Caricature Salon of 1846*, he had delighted in carnivalizing the establishment, and the slightly ironic and mocking tone of certain pieces of the 1857 edition of *Les Fleurs du mal* attest to his continued use of such tactics. But in 1857 his past caught up with him: on 20 August the Sixth Correctional Tribunal of Paris found him guilty of committing an "affront to public morality and common decency." Six of the poems from *Les Fleurs du mal* were condemned, and the sale of any collection containing these reportedly obscene pieces was strictly forbidden.

Although the repressive measures of the Second Empire did serve to infuriate the poet, they also backfired predictably, for Baudelaire drew sudden and substantial attention. The *Madame Bovary* trial had piqued public interest in such matters, and copies of the *Fleurs* saved from confiscation sold briskly under the counter at twice their cover price.[2]

---

1. There was considerable speculation that Louis Napoleon was the product of an illicit liaison (Thompson, 5–6); but more important, his disregard for the constitution and his institution of an authoritarian regime while disguising it with republican structures (the Senate, for example), left his authority on uneven footing. Riding on the coattails of the empire, he regularly demonstrated that he fell far short of his uncle. Marx was not the only one to see him as a farcical repetition of the earlier regime; see Goldstein, 172–76.

2. For additional background on the censorship, see Pommier, 93.

Yet aside from providing the short-term windfall benefits commonly occasioned by such a *succès de scandale*,[3] the censorship of *Les Fleurs du mal* hit Baudelaire where it hurt, sentencing him to selective silence, even—or especially—in matters concerning his own case: article 17 of the press law of 1852 prohibited discussion in the press of censorship cases.[4] It would be naive to think that even Baudelaire—who had more than his share of impertinence—would remain unaffected when working under a gag order that threatened his very livelihood. The efficacy of the Second Empire's censorship might therefore be measured by its value as *deterrent*, by its ability to prevent future abuses.

At first glance, one might suppose the legal reprimand to have been effective in Baudelaire's case. The project the poet pursued after the completion of the *Fleurs*,[5] the prose poems posthumously collected as *Spleen de Paris* (1869), drew no attention from the censors. In fact, as they appeared sporadically through the 1860s, none of the poems seems to have been refused publication for political reasons, even though many literary journals were practicing a form of prophylactic self-censorship that would have induced them to steer clear of the pariah Baudelaire had become.[6] In many ways, Baudelaire seems to have decided to "play it safe." Suppressing any sign of the daring sexuality of the condemned pieces, he had adopted what might be considered the less alienating and arguably more plebian language of prose, and had engaged in the sterile activity of repeating in prosaic, "watered-down" versions poems from

3.   The tangible benefits for Baudelaire were few however, for the condemnation included a fine of three hundred francs. After lengthy negotiations he managed to have the sum reduced to fifty francs.

4.   "It is forbidden to report on trials for press infractions. The prosecution alone may be announced; in every case the verdict will be published," (Duvergier, vol. 52). This is why the articles written by D'Aurevilly and Asselineau in support of the *Fleurs du mal* were available to the court only in the form of the *articles justificatifs* (supporting documents) Baudelaire himself had had printed; it is also why Baudelaire was threatened with legal action a second time for having discussed Flaubert's legal battle (and by implication his own) in an article on *Madame Bovary*.

5.   Indeed, he had already begun to dabble in prose poetry: "La Solitude" was written in 1855; "L'Horloge," "L'invitation au voyage," and "Un hémisphère dans une chevelure" in 1857.

6.   It was just this kind of unofficial blacklisting that led the *Revue contemporaine* to shun "Le Cygne" in 1859. Five of the prose poems were refused by the *Revue Nationale et Etrangère* in 1865, although the refusal does not seem to have been politically motivated. On the practice of journalistic self-censorship, see Bellet, 24–30.

the *Fleurs*, those already deemed "harmless" by the censors.[7] In 1861 he even courted the establishment, angling for a seat on the staid Académie française.

A first glance, however, is never enough. As the saying goes, appearances can be deceiving, and in a Baudelairean esthetic that privileges the jubilant power of surprise, they are made to be so. Seemingly innocuous, even conformist, activities bore a subversive underside. Just as his campaign for the Académie française was something of a spoof (he referred to it as his *candidature bouffonne* [*Correspondance*, 2:580]), the seemingly anodyne and anecdotal prose poems can often be shown to include corrosive attacks on the dominant culture. However, these attacks only become apparent with a second glance, one from a different perspective; the anecdotal components of the poems actually deflect the reader's attention from the attacks that they mask. Unlike traditional allegory, which aims for harmony between levels, in the prose poems Baudelaire frequently makes poetry operate on multiple, often *incompatible* registers, so that one reading appears to invalidate another. In so doing, he refines his esthetics of allegory, capitalizing on the dual nature he had earlier ascribed to all beauty.[8]

The brilliance of Baudelaire's refined allegory is that it is *ironical*: that is, it resists identifying itself as allegory; it conceals its own figurality[9]—a

---

7. Baudelaire fretted about the lack of originality of the prose poems in his correspondence, seeing them alternately as a reheated serving of *Les Fleurs du mal* or as the second panel of his poetic diptych.

8. Always of two minds, Baudelaire plays alternately on techniques of harmony ("Correspondances" [1857]) and of juxtaposition ("Une charogne" [1857]). As early as the *Salon de 1846* Baudelaire had insisted on the coupling of the eternal and the transitory in modern art (*Oeuvres*, 2:493), yet he also complained of artists who had adhered to such a principle (*Oeuvres*, 2:558; see Hannoosh, 152–78). By the time of *Le Peintre de la vie moderne* (1863), Baudelaire insists on the importance of an "irreducible dualism" in the work of Constantin Guys (*Oeuvres*, 2:685, 689). It would appear that in his later work (and especially in the prose poems—themselves a generic juxtaposition) Baudelaire marks a preference for the dualistic conception of allegory. The turning point, as Benjamin has suggested, is "Le Cygne," which dates from 1859, two years after the trial. Baudelaire's gradual privileging of doubleness is not exclusively esthetic; it also affords certain political advantages, as we shall see. (For more on the importance of this poem in Baudelaire's esthetics, see Burton, 149–69.)

9. Baudelaire's artful exploitation of irony as a screen from the authorities recalls Flaubert's defense in the *Madame Bovary* trial. Dominick LaCapra has shown that if the novelist won his legal battle over *Madame Bovary*, it was largely because the prosecution could not show how the book was to be read. In

strategy with obvious and multiple applications under the repressive regime of the Second Empire. Silenced by the law, Baudelaire finds a way to speak, but "mutely," as it were. Moreover, these "silent allegories" subvert the restrictions on expression *doubly*: they reflect upon censorship all the while operating *under its pall*. This, as we shall see, is the narrative mode of subversion.

In *Spleen de Paris* the strategy of ironic masking has been methodically developed, the irony so refined that the reader often languishes in ambiguity. The repetitions (of earlier poems and of set expressions,[10] etc.) that constitute the collection walk a fine line: repetition is the first step toward banality and cliché; however, it is also the vehicle of irony. In a sense, the novelty of *Spleen de Paris* consists of the way Baudelaire manipulates irony, making it masquerade as banality in astonishing ways.

Baudelaire's aggressive poetry constitutes a "counterpart" (what he called in his correspondence a *pendant*) to *Les Fleurs du mal* in part because it does more than repeat elements of *Les Fleurs du mal*. In many ways it analyzes the earlier collection *in its effects*, in the specific terms of its public and legal reception. A simple example is found in the piece "Le Chien et le flacon" ("The Dog and the Flask," 1862), in which the poet compares a dog's preference for excrement instead of perfume to the poor taste of the general public (*Oeuvres*, 1:284). Here one finds a reworking of the earlier collection; the mention of perfume metonymically evokes flowers; in particular, flowers found distasteful by the public, like *Les Fleurs du mal* themselves. More specifically it evokes "Le Flacon" ("The Flask," 1857), a poem from the earlier collection, where the comparison between poetry and perfume is also made. But "Le Chien et le flacon" does not limit itself to repetition. What it adds to the earlier poem is precisely "le chien," that insipid public, more taken with doggerel than with exquisite verse, for whom Baudelaire, in exasperation, found himself writing. "I could not resist the desire to please my contemporaries," he wrote in his notes for a preface to the 1861 edition, "as can be seen in the few bits of garbage

---

short, it was unclear to the court whether the novel constituted an *attack* on bourgeois values, or whether it *upheld* those values by showing the plight of those who fail to abide by them (LaCapra, 30–52).

10. On some uses of cliché expressions in the prose poems, see Barbara Johnson, *Défigurations*, chap. 4.

written in hopes of getting the misery of my subject excused. But our fine journalists did not appreciate the affection I showed them, and I have thus purged any trace of it" (*Oeuvres*, 1:184).[11]

Now the allegorical operation of "Le chien et le flacon" is relatively transparent; to the extent that one recognizes the sarcastic jab at the public, the anecdote has not masked the subtext. But in this light poem, little is at stake; the poet risks nothing more than rattling bourgeois sensibilities. But what becomes of Baudelaire's allegory when the stakes are raised? After all, his attacks went beyond facile sniping at the public. The extent to which he engaged himself in the struggle against the dominant culture, and the extent to which this struggle situated itself in the vehicle of dominance that is language, can best be seen in the poem that "Le Chien et le flacon" precedes and, one might say, introduces: "Le Mauvais Vitrier" ("The Bad Glazier," 1862; *Oeuvres*, 1:285–87).[12]

This curious little piece, perhaps the most enigmatic of the entire collection, proposes to analyze the phenomenon of unmotivated actions:

Il y a des natures purement contemplatives et tout à fait impropres à l'action, qui cependant, *sous une impulsion mystérieuse et inconnue*, agissent quelquefois avec une rapidité dont elles se seraient crues elles-mêmes incapables.

(There are people of a purely contemplative nature, wholly unsuited to action, who nevertheless, *under a mysterious and unknown impulse*, sometimes act with a speed of which they would have believed themselves incapable.)

In support of his thesis the poet offers a series of examples: a harmless dreamer one day sets fire to a forest, a friend lights up a cigar next to a powder keg, an unusually timid soul suddenly plants a kiss on an old man in the street. The narrator himself is not immune to this kind of outburst, and he relates in detail his encounter one day with a street-going glazier.

11. All translations are my own. In the case of the quotation of poetry, the original will be given with the translation.

12. For readers unfamiliar with the text it has been included in its entirety in the Appendix. Perhaps because it so steadfastly refuses to be domesticated by interpretation, or because the allusion to glaziers in the preface grants this piece privileged status, "Le Mauvais Vitrier" has become something of a test case for interpretive approaches to the prose poems. See Pizzorusso, Heck, Toumayan (78–90), Ido, Murphy.

After maliciously inviting the merchant to climb the six flights leading to his garret, the poet maligns his wares, scandalized that the glazier has only clear glass:

> "Comment? vous n'avez pas de verres de couleur? des verres roses, rouges, bleus, des vitres magiques, des vitres de paradis? Impudent que vous êtes! vous osez vous promener dans des quartiers pauvres, et vous n'avez pas même de vitres qui fassent voir la vie en beau!"

> (What? You have no colored glass? No pink glass, nor red, nor blue? No magic panes, panes of paradise? How could you be so impudent! You dare to walk through impoverished neighborhoods, and you don't even carry panes that might make life beautiful!)

After pushing the peddler back down the stairs, the narrator awaits his reappearance from the doorway below, whereupon he bombards his unsuspecting victim with a flowerpot. As he listens to the shatter of glass he muses,

> Ces plaisanteries nerveuses ne sont pas sans péril, et on peut souvent les payer cher. Mais qu'importe l'éternité de la damnation à qui a trouvé dans une seconde l'infini de la jouissance?

> (These spirited jokes are not without their dangers, and one often pays dearly for them. But what does an eternity of damnation matter to one who has found, in a single second, the boundlessness of pleasure?)

What *does* it matter? The rhetorical question concluding the poem begs for an answer. Indeed, one of the reasons this poem has drawn upon itself considerable critical attention is that it thematically asserts its own inexplicability, thereby throwing down the gauntlet to the reader. As if to render the piece entirely inscrutable, the narrator underscores, in each example, the *arbitrary* nature of the outbursts he has witnessed or experienced. The acts seem altogether unmotivated—so lacking in intent that attempts to ascribe stimuli amount to a grasping at straws:

> Un autre allumera un cigare à côté d'un tonneau de poudre, *pour voir, pour savoir, pour tenter la destinée*, pour se contraindre lui-même à faire preuve d'énergie, pour faire le joueur, pour connaître

les plaisirs de l'anxiété, pour rien, par caprice, par désoeuvrement. (emphasis in original)

(Another will light up a cigar next to a powder keg, *to see, to find out, to tempt fate*, to make a show of strength, to play the gambler, to experience the pleasures of anxiety, for no reason, because of a whim, out of boredom.)

This dismantling of causality removes the incident from the jurisdiction of positivist discourse, which, as in science and law, strives to trace causes to effects. Here, "Le moraliste et le médecin, qui prétendent tout savoir, ne peuvent pas expliquer d'où vient si subitement une si folle énergie" (The moralist and the physician, who claim to know everything, cannot explain whence comes so suddenly such a mad energy). The lack of causal explanation thus prompts the narrator to cast the poem in the terms of a frame that specifically plays on inconsistencies in physical laws: the supernatural. What is first referred to as a "mysterious impulse" becomes a "mad energy," then to be incarnated as "malicious Demons" who enter us and lead to our ultimate damnation by their "satanic inspiration."

It is hardly surprising that Baudelaire should invoke the supernatural; after all, it was he who had introduced Edgar Allan Poe to the French, and one of Poe's stories, "The Imp of the Perverse," provided considerable inspiration for "Le Mauvais Vitrier" (see Pizzorusso).[13] However, if Baudelaire rides on the coattails of the fantastic, it is less from incidental influence than because the genre offers special features he wants to exploit. Most of all, it would appear to guarantee the absence of any *political* content. Of primary importance is the fact that the supernatural suspends or inverts the normal march of chronology; the timelessness of spirits and of the human psyche distance such tales from the concerns of any particular historical moment. Also, while literature of the supernatural may be in some sense subversive, its subversion resides on the level of the *personal* rather than the *social*. Stories of phantoms, doubles, and animated objects undermine a reader's complacency about an essentially predictable and controllable world. In fantastic literature, the subgenre that capitalizes on what might be called the "dark" super-

13. Indeed, the spirit of perversion so central to "Le Mauvais Vitrier" runs through a number of Poe's tales, translated by Baudelaire in 1857 as *Nouvelles Histoires extraordinaires*.

natural, the supernatural intervenes to replace causality with analogy and to suggest that the recesses of the unconscious provide access to a parallel and frighteningly private world, one in which individuals are subjugated by irrational laws.

As Todorov has shown (35), the fantastic is largely characterized by the hesitation it provokes in the reader between real and supernatural interpretations; the reader is made ill-at-ease by the suspicion that something has eluded the cold light of reason, and that invisible rifts in the texture of the ordinary world may in fact exist. If "Le Mauvais Vitrier" triggers something akin to this malaise, it is because the text is, in a sense, "haunted," and not just by the demons the narrator mentions. As we shall soon see, there is another story, so diaphanous as to be nearly invisible, that circulates within the text like a ghost. The reader, who remains unable to discern the ghost clearly, finds it nevertheless profoundly unsettling.

As if to highlight that even the uncaused causes of the fantastic have their effects, the poet insists, at the end of the poem, on *consequences*: "These spirited jokes are not without their dangers," he remarked, "and one often pays dearly for them." The poem is thus caught in a tension between a demonstration of cause and effect (penalties incurred by malicious acts) and a disavowal of causality (the invocation of the supernatural). The tension is even evident in a certain quirkiness in Baudelaire's language. Specifically at the moment of demonic possession, when one might presume causality to have reached its nadir, words of some consequence appear in unusual contexts. Such is the case when, after sending away the beleaguered glazier, the poet plots a further attack:

> Je m'approchai du balcon et je me saisis d'un petit pot de fleurs, et quand l'homme reparut au débouché de la porte, je laissai tomber perpendiculairement mon engin de guerre sur le rebord postérieur de ses crochets; et le choc le renversant, il acheva de briser sous son dos toute sa pauvre fortune ambulatoire qui rendit le bruit éclatant d'un palais de cristal crevé par la foudre.

> (I approached the balcony and picked up a small pot of flowers, and when the fellow reappeared from the doorway below, I dropped my war machine perpendicularly upon the back edge of his peddler's pack; the shock knocked him over, and he thoroughly shattered under his back his entire poor, ambulatory fortune, which made the resounding noise of a crystal palace struck by lightning.)

As if to add ballast to an already substantial bomb, Baudelaire invokes the cumbersome adverb "perpendiculairement," "perpendicularly"—so ponderous and unlyrical that Littré cites only technical uses. This word falls outside Baudelaire's standard poetic lexicon; in fact, it seems to occur in only one other place in all of his work, the third sketch for a preface to *Les Fleurs du mal* (c. 1862), where he maintains that

> la phrase poétique peut imiter... la ligne horizontale, la ligne droite ascendante, la ligne droite descendante; elle peut monter à pic vers le ciel, sans essoufflement, ou descendre *perpendiculairement* vers l'enfer avec la vélocité de toute pesanteur. (*Oeuvres* 1:183)

> (the poetic phrase can imitate the horizontal line, the straight ascending line, the straight descending line; it can rise steeply toward the sky, without strain, or descend *perpendicularly* toward hell with all the weight of gravity.)

The recurrence of the word "perpendiculairement" gives the reader an angle on just what kind of ghost is lurking within "Le Mauvais Vitrier": the flowerpot plummeting toward the glazier follows the same trajectory as—and is thus in some measure akin to—the poetic phrase.[14] But what "poetic phrase" could be so gratuitous as the launching of this *engin de guerre*? Only poetic phrases that are entirely unmotivated could meet this description, phrases that set as their goal nothing less than the creation of Beauty, either ex nihilo, or by transformation of the mundane. It is no accident, then, that this transformatory power is precisely what the narrator misses in the glazier's prosaic wares: "Comment? vous n'avez pas de verres de couleur? des verres roses, rouges, bleus?" The felicitous substitution here of *verres* ("glass") for the more standard *vitres* ("panes") reinforces, by its homophonic evocation of poetic "verse" (*vers*), the narrator's commitment to a transformatory poetry (see Pizzorusso, 169), the kind that can turn a terra cotta pot into a "war machine" and a glazier's wares into a vulnerable "crystal palace." In this light, the glazier and his transparent goods become an emblem of prosaic clarity, of the supposedly limpid, cliché-ridden discourse of everyday life.

A poetic esthetic that aims for the creation of absolute beauty would seem insulated from the concerns of a workaday world. One might say

14. Kaplan (46) also comments on the oddity of this word.

that it would exist merely for its own sake, which is, of course, the essence of the Parnassian program of Art for Art's Sake, in which artistic creation is as gratuitous and as free of ulterior motives as, for example, the inexplicable outbursts related in "Le Mauvais Vitrier."

The parallel between these outbursts and such lyric esthetics as Art for Art's Sake invites the reader to view "Le Mauvais Vitrier" as a poem that is somehow "about" poetry.[15] As such, the unmotivated acts (setting fires, dropping pots, etc.) could be seen as a staging of the poetic operation itself, in which poetry is construed as gratuitous violence wrought upon reality. Violent transformations are certainly in accord with Baudelaire's alchemical, nearly supernatural view of poetry, which specifically entailed the conversion of grim banality into beauty: "Tu m'as donné ta boue," he wrote in the projected epilogue to *Les Fleurs du mal*, "et j'en ai fait de l'or" (You gave me your mud and I turned it into gold) (*Oeuvres*, 1:192). "Le Mauvais Vitrier" demonstrates just such violence and metamorphosis. Thus, dropping the flowerpot destroys the commonplace, the vulgar, transparent panes; however, at the same time, it results in the creation of beauty, presumably in the form of the prismatic spectrum of color emanating from shards of broken glass.

The impact of the pot is also the impact of the poetic phrase upon hackneyed, pedestrian language, as epitomized by cliché. Amossy and Rosen have described the cliché as a *figure usée* (17), a "worn-down figure"; that is, a figure whose figurality is no longer recognized and that is used as indexical language. In "Le Mauvais Vitrier," the cliché functions as a kind of "sleeper," an *agent provocateur* that travels "*mis*cognito," giving itself as pure designation, but whose figurality can be activated at any time. Acting as an *inspiration satanique* (satanic inspiration), poetic inspiration breathes new life into dead figures, which the vignettes in the first half of the poem exemplify: setting ablaze the forest corresponds to the cliché expression *jouer avec le feu* (playing with fire), lighting up cigars by powder kegs evokes *mettre le feu aux poudres* (to light a powder keg, meaning to touch off a crisis), and the accosting of a stranger in the street conjures up the image of a Romantic embrace of the unknown.[16] Plundering the dictionary of its most hackneyed expressions—

15. Baudelaire's own relationship with the esthetics of Art for Art's Sake is problematic. See his essay on Pierre Dupont (2:26–36).

16. See the end of "Le Voyage" (significantly, it is the last line of the last work of the collection): "Plonger ... au fond de l'Inconnu pour trouver *du nouveau*" (Plunge into the depths of the Unknown to find *something new*) (*Oeuvres*, 1:134).

expressions rendered by usage as transparent as plate glass—Baudelaire produces poetry.[17]

Yet the final scene, that of the poet's encounter with the glazier, suggests that poetic production, however unmotivated, is not without its consequences. Satanic inspiration, appropriately enough, can lead to eternal damnation: "But what does an eternity of damnation matter to one who has found in a second the boundlessness of pleasure?" Eternal damnation, which is a punishment usually associated with moral depravity rather than with mere delinquency, may seem rather stiff reparation for the breakage of a few panes of glass. That is, until one reads this scene, too, as the resurrection of a hackneyed expression, and one that places the poet's attack squarely in the domain of morality. *Casser les vitres*, "breaking windows," appears in the lexicon as a cliché figure for "creating scandal."

The story of this scandal is the "ghost" that haunts Baudelaire's text. Just what the scandal might consist of becomes clear in the poet's correspondence. In 1857, as he awaited his trial, he wrote his mother: "I beg you to consider this *scandal* (which is causing a real stir in Paris) as nothing more than the foundation of my fortune" (*Correspondance*, 1:419). In the introduction to the documents he had submitted to the courts, he spoke of the "spiritualité *éclatante*" (shattering/dazzling playfulness) of *Les Fleurs du mal* (*Oeuvres*, 1:193). By 1859, as he prepared the new, augmented edition of the collection, he reveled in its explosive power, writing to Poulet-Malassis: "Nouvelles *Fleurs du mal* faites. *A tout casser, comme une explosion de gaz chez un vitrier*" (New *Fleurs du mal* finished. Enough to shatter everything, like a gas explosion at a glazier's) (*Correspondance*, 1:568). Although the act of throwing flowers (*jeter des fleurs*) is customarily a complimentary gesture (roughly equivalent to showering someone with praise), the flowers in "Le Mauvais Vitrier" appear strangely malevolent. They are, in fact, "window breaking," scandalous; none other than the collection of flowers (and blossoms are implied in the words *anthologie* and *florilège*) known as *Les Fleurs du mal*.[18] This is the bomb Baudelaire had dared to drop for the sake of dropping it, which had caused such a scandal, and for which a

---

17. On the literalization, or "defiguring" of figurative language, see Johnson (*Défigurations*, chap. 4). On Baudelaire's debt to Grandville see Hannoosh, 158–72.

18. *Florilège*, from the Latin for flower; the Greek *anthos* (in *antho*logie) refers to blossoms as well. See Kaplan, 46.

price had had to be paid. It resulted not in the *damnation éternelle* evoked in "Le Mauvais Vitrier," but in the legal *condamnation* of Baudelaire and his work.

Just what has Baudelaire done in this piece? In encoded form he has repeated the shocking gesture of the publication of *Les Fleurs du mal*. At the same time he outlines his poetic program: since the gas explosion in the letter to Poulet-Malassis refers particularly to the *new* poems, Baudelaire now seems to be setting out deliberately to break some windows. While the original *Fleurs du mal* created scandal unintentionally, the later poems set out to unsettle bourgeois complacency. This intent was to manifest itself in a deliberate practice of destabilization, demonstrable in Baudelaire's strategic uses of incongruities. Thus, in "Le Mauvais Vitrier," the victim becomes the glazier who, although apparently more compatible with the gallery of characters with whom Baudelaire usually sympathizes (the ragpicker, the prostitute, etc.), here represents the dominant culture. The glazier not only embodies one of Baudelaire's scapegoats, Arsène Houssaye, as Steve Murphy has shown; he also emblematizes, more generally, the bourgeois. The transformation of the glazier's wares into a *palais de cristal* (palace of crystal) makes of him the walking advertisement for a commercialized midcentury society whose goods were displayed in galleries and exposition halls, the most famous of which was London's Crystal Palace (see Murphy, 346; Benjamin, 36). The preference of the bourgeois for transparency, and thus his resistance to the change engendered by a *vitre magique*, signals his interest in perpetuating the status quo. As Geraldine Friedman writes, "ideology promotes the fiction of a transparent relation between language and the world" (317), and it is precisely this presupposed transparency that Baudelaire was to call into question.

In his attack on the glazier, Baudelaire repeats his original affront to society. This time, however, he works in the mode of irony. Rather than taunt bourgeois morality with explicit provocations (as in *Les Fleurs du mal*), Baudelaire attempts here to undermine the self-assuredness that subtends the bourgeois viewpoint. His approach does not lead, in "Le Mauvais Vitrier," to a demonstration of the self-interest of moral perspectives (although such a demonstration *is* the stake in such a piece as "Le Joujou des pauvres" [The plaything of the poor, 1862]); instead, Baudelaire works at a more elemental level. Setting his sights on the reader for whom, for example, the condemned poems from *Les Fleurs du mal* were "obviously," or "clearly," or "transparently" immoral, he seeks to challenge the assumptions that allow such self-assured intransigence to obtain. His approach consists of shattering the very idea of transparency: by arousing the figure that lies dormant within the cliché and by contaminating positivist discourse with the fantastic, Baudelaire undermines that notion of univocal language upon which authority depends.

The attack, however, is accomplished with impunity. Baudelaire's "trick" is to write subversion out in the open, to exploit what appears to be the prosaic language of the dominant discourse. The subversive agenda is cloaked in a "harmless" anecdote, rendered all the more innocuous by its leanings toward the fantastic. The anecdote is allegorical, but it is an *ironic allegory*: allegory because it represents metaphorically the whole scenario of the *Fleurs du mal* case, but ironic because the text *seems* to be telling no allegory at all. Indeed, the irony *masks* the allegory. Baudelaire thus counts on (and protects himself by) the ideological blindness of his reader: the bourgeois who refuses to identify with the glazier remains a witness to the victimization of his counterpart, whom he will always mistake for *somebody else.*

Yet it should not be supposed that "Le Mauvais Vitrier" represents an exercise in sterility; its disruptive power is not entirely eclipsed by its innocuous anecdote. The levels of the narrative do not explicitly interact, as they would, say, in traditional allegory, but the fundamental ambiguity of the poem makes itself felt. The unresolved tensions between hazard and causality, between the narrator and the glazier, between nature and the supernatural, suffice to render the poem profoundly unsettling. The bourgeois reader who may sense something familiar, but without recognizing what, in the resurrection of cliché expressions, or even in the floral attack against the glazier, is experiencing a disruption in what he would like to consider domesticated, univocal language. In short, there is a demon in the system. This demon, invoked as the "malicious Demons" and the "satanic inspiration" that subvert normal causality, is, ironically, that very link with supernatural literature that had at first seemed to neutralize the social content of "Le Mauvais Vitrier," limiting it to the personal terrors of the ghost story.

Yet the genres of the supernatural introduce—in however fragmentary a form—a parallel world, along with its malicious interference with our supposedly stable reality. This parallelism of worlds, or of readings, clearly partakes of metaphor and allegory. Thus, the supernatural power that erupts within this text is precisely the demonic and irrepressible force of rhetoric. Metaphor interferes with univocal discourse, and it does so in what is both the most strategic and the most common of places: the commonplace. Cliché, which is at once designation *and* figure (yet not completely either), resides at the nexus between parallel worlds, between the platitudes of the literal and the demonic world of the figurative. Often used as pure designation, cliché holds in reserve a figure that may at any moment be awakened. The spirit of perversion so delightfully depicted by Baudelaire aims for this activation, this perversion of the cliché from its "normal usage." The interference it creates (here, its suggestion of an alternative reality and reading) implies an ideological threat: it challenges the supposed "naturalness" and transparency of the dominant discourse. Moreover, the fantastic traditionally elicits a hesitation on the part of the reader, who straddles natural and supernatural explanations (Todorov, 35). This hesitation, due to the intransigent ambiguity of Baudelaire's tale, further undermines the authority and univocity of the dominant culture, represented in "Le Mauvais Vitrier" by the confounded "moralist" and "physician."

The sensitivity of "Le Mauvais Vitrier" to the duplicity of cliché, to the ambiguity of the fantastic, and to the divisiveness of classes, serves to underscore another duality: that incarnated by the poet himself—the kind of doubleness Nerval had already put to good use, as we saw in Chapter 4. The acerbic subtlety of Baudelaire's poetic assault upon the dominant culture could come only from an outsider who also has an inside view. Although Baudelaire had never mixed well with the mainstream of bourgeois society, it was the legal defeat in the *Fleurs du mal* case that rendered his social eccentricity official. The public reprimand had come with a fine that plunged the poet further into debt. More to the point, the imperial decree of 2 February 1852, which deprived criminals of their voting rights, moved Baudelaire into the ranks of the marginal citizen (see Pommier, 97). Living on the "edge," as it were, Baudelaire straddled the inside and the outside; he could be, in the words of "Les Foules" (Crowds, 1861) both "himself and others" (*Oeuvres*, 1:291). Yet his splintered identity was not so anodyne as it may appear: Baudelaire occupied, as Ross Chambers has pointed out, the role of the parasite.

Parasites find themselves in an irreducibly ambivalent position, both harmful to and dependent upon their hosts, and the *Spleen de Paris* is filled with images of this kind of mutually destructive relationship. We have seen how, in "Le Mauvais Vitrier," Baudelaire cast bourgeois society in the form of a merchant bearing a *palais de cristal*, and the poet's destruction of this Crystal Palace evokes an attack on the very galleries and expositions that so fascinated him (Benjamin, Chapter 2). Moreover, the very notion of a poetry-in-prose might suggest a genre that feeds off the banalities of bourgeois language, but that in so doing destroys this banality. Certainly this is what happens to cliché in "Le Mauvais Vitrier," where Baudelaire's handling of such expressions as "casser les vitres" confers strangeness and opacity upon what had formerly been reduced to seemingly transparent usage.[19]

The alienation of common usage is one of the esthetic devices standard to the prose poems, and Baudelaire regularly focuses on cliché and proverb in order to reveal the realities that these supposedly transparent expressions blind us to. Thus, in "Les Dons des fées" ("The fairies' gifts," 1862; *Oeuvres*, 1:305–7), he stages the expression "les fées se sont penchées sur son berceau" (the fairies visited his cradle), a proverbial explanation for someone who has led a charmed life. While the presence of fairies would seem, like the demons in "Le Mauvais Vitrier," to sever the links between cause and effect, thus associating good fortune with what might appear to be an ideologically neutral notion of chance, Baudelaire takes pains to show that good luck has nothing to do with happenstance. The rich get richer, the poor poorer:

> Ainsi la puissance d'attirer magnétiquement la fortune fut adjugée à l'héritier unique d'une famille très-riche, qui, n'étant doué d'aucun sens de charité, non plus que d'aucune convoitise pour les biens les plus visibles de la vie, devait se trouver plus tard prodigieusement embarrassé de ses millions.
>
> Ainsi furent donnés l'amour du Beau et la Puissance poétique au fils d'un sombre gueux, carrier de son état, qui ne pouvait, en aucune façon aider les facultés, ni soulager les besoins de sa déplorable progéniture.

> Thus the power to attract fortune magnetically was awarded to the sole heir of a very rich family, who, not endowed with any sense of charity, nor with any desire for the most apparent luxuries of life, was destined to find himself later prodigiously encumbered by his millions.
>
> Thus were granted poetic power and the love of Beauty to the son of a gloomy ne'er-do-well, a quarry laborer, who could in no way nurture the abilities, nor ease the needs of his deplorable offspring.

19. "Specifically, by turning the language of dominant discourse *against itself*, the prose poem devised a strategy for counter-discourse which could begin to situate the oppressive character of the dominant itself" (Terdiman, 270). Friedman, too, identifies cliché with the voice of ideology (323).

None of those in attendance view the blatant inequities of distribution as unusual. Their indifference is perhaps not so surprising as it might appear, for such a distribution mirrors the platitudes of a Christian morality that regularly placates the poor by the promise of spiritual gifts, holding out the carrot of an important inheritance for the meek, or by exaggerating the hurdles confronting the rich in their ascent toward heaven. So, in "Les Dons des fées," the judgments proceed as if they were normal—at least, until the rigorous distinction between classes is breached. When a petit bourgeois shopkeeper finds his son left, because of an oversight, with a *spiritual* gift, the *don de plaire* ("the talent to please") it clashes with his sense of material entitlement, and he is profoundly vexed: "Mais plaire comment? plaire . . . ? plaire pourquoi?" (But please in what way? please . . . ? please, but whatever for?) (*Oeuvres*, 1:307).

Baudelaire's plays on commonplaces such as "les fées se sont penchées sur son berceau" estrange everyday language. But the strangeness is less one that Baudelaire gratuitously invests in these expressions than one he rouses and points out to the reader. Putting clichés and proverbs on the stage, making them *perform*, shows that they are neither so lifeless nor so neutral as they appear to be. The "standard" usage of language often serves to perpetuate the structures and concerns of the dominant culture, and Baudelaire shows how language can act as both a symptom and an instrument of bourgeois blindness. Thus, in "Un Plaisant" (A buffoon, 1862) when an elegantly attired gentleman tips his hat to a whipped and harried donkey, and wishes it a Happy New Year ("Je vous la souhaite bonne et heureuse!" [*Oeuvres*, 1:279]), he is blithely oblivious to the fact that he is addressing a pack animal, and one whose new year promises to be as unhappy as the last. The holiday greeting simply glosses over differences in station and ignores that there is a population for which such a salutation is grossly out of place.

The prose poems thus demonstrate how the linguistic commonplace acts as a gesture of exclusion, and how language can be seen to have its victims. Nowhere are these lessons more apparent than in "Une mort héroïque" ("An heroic death," 1863 [*Oeuvres*, 1:319-23]), another poem patterned after a tale by Poe ("Hop Frog"), and in many ways a complement to "Le Mauvais Vitrier." If "Le Mauvais Vitrier" can be viewed as a reenactment of the scandal resulting from Baudelaire's new poetic *phrase*, then "Une mort héroïque" deals with the impact of the legal *sentence*.

That this sentence is what is at stake, however, is obscured by the broad outlines of the story. An actor, Fancioulle, is arrested for leading a conspiracy against an unidentified Prince, and he is sentenced to death. A slight hope for reprieve is tendered: the conspirator is to perform for his life. In the midst of a dazzling and properly death-defying spectacle, the Prince's page blows a whistle from the back of the crowd, and Fancioulle, startled from the reverie of his role, gasps, stumbles, and expires on stage.

As in "Le Mauvais Vitrier" Baudelaire has managed to write, in the guise of a single anecdote, two stories that are directly contradictory. The first of these seems to recount how power is affirmed by repression: a dictator props up his reign by the public execution of conspirators. This overtly political poem had, as Peter Schofer has described, a historical referent, and one that could have made of it a fable entirely palatable to the government of the Second Empire: it loosely follows the lines of the Orsini affair of 1858 (Schofer, 50–52; Wing, 3–4). Condemned for an assassination plot against the emperor, Felice Orsini made for spectacular "theater" of a grisly sort, throughout a highly publicized trial and right up to the victim's cries of "Vive l'Italie, vive la France" on the scaffold before his execution (Schofer, 51). Viewed as a thinly veiled allegory, in which the Italian resonance of the name Fancioulle and the use of the imperial title "Prince" help keep the story on its rails, "Une mort héroïque" illustrates the reinforcement of despotic power.

However, the text repeatedly calls attention to the *strangeness* of the terms of its own allegorization, which conjoins politics and esthetics.[20] Thus the narrator comments explicitly on the unusual linkage:

> bien qu'il puisse paraître bizarre que les idées de patrie et de liberté s'emparent despotiquement du cerveau d'un histrion, un jour Fancioulle entra dans une conspiration formée par quelques gentilshommes mécontents.

> (although it may seem bizarre that the ideas of freedom and country could take a despotic hold on the mind of a thespian, one day Fancioulle entered into a conspiracy formed by a few unhappy gentlemen.)

20. For an examination of the text's uncomfortable handling of this mixture of art and politics, see, again, Schofer, 53–57. Schofer's suggestion that "power ... destroys great art" (54) reflects one of the "stories" being recounted. However, as we shall see, Baudelaire ultimately reverses the terms, showing how art destroys power.

Likewise, in lieu of the guillotine (which had been Orsini's predictable destination), the instrument of Fancioulle's demise is "un coup de sifflet," the blow of a whistle, the equivalent of a jeer. Here political execution takes the form of *esthetic* disapproval, although both fates are implied. The "coup de sifflet," which is "as swift as a sword," cuts two ways. It results in a staging of the figure "couper le sifflet à quelqu'un," which can mean both cutting someone's throat (as the guillotine did for Orsini), or cutting someone off in speech ("couper la parole," "interloquer"). Fancioulle feels both prongs of the figure: his death comes from a jeer that reduces him to silence.

Now political silencing was a practice Baudelaire knew something about, and he was keenly attuned to the theatricality associated with such events. That he saw the *Fleurs du mal* trial as a kind of play-acting, in which his own elaborate preparations collided with a previously scripted verdict, was evident from his report afterward to Flaubert: "We acted out our little comedy on Friday," he wrote after his court appearance (*Correspondance*, 1:424). Participating in the debate on the regulation of speech, "Une mort héroïque" repeatedly describes the Prince's despotism in terms of censorship, remarking, for example, that a "harsh" historian might have referred to the despot as a monster, "if one were allowed, in his kingdom, to write anything that was not designed exclusively for pleasure or surprise.'[21] Similarly, after Fancioulle's demise, his fellow conspirators are "erased [*effacés*] from life," like so many words rubbed out by the imperial censor.

All this attention to language helps the reader to recast the scenario of a political conspiracy (*conspiration*) into the terms of a poetic *inspiration*, with the subsequent denunciation being the work not of the "good citizens" who blew the whistle on Fancioulle, but rather of a few partisan journalists of the *Figaro*: those who had drawn attention to Baudelaire in 1857 (see Pichois' note in *Oeuvres*, 1:1177). A reading that follows this vein unravels the implicit moral of the Orsini affair, which had seemed to reassert the supremacy of the empire. During his final performance, Fancioulle is certainly guilty of usurping the power of the Prince; the spectacle proves more despotic than the despot himself, who, enthralled by the actor's art, finds himself reduced to nothing more than a member of *le public*, the audience. It is hardly surprising that his vengeful re-

21. The link between the censorship of Fancioulle and that of Baudelaire has been noted and developed in different directions by Starobinski (*Portrait de l'artiste*, 85–90, and Wing, 9).

sponse to the situation takes the form of an execution, but it results in an unexpected twist as the epilogue recounts Fancioulle's fate in terms of a *favor* bestowed upon the victim:

> Depuis lors, plusieurs mimes, justement appréciés dans différ-ents pays, sont venus jouer devant la cour de ***; mais aucun d'eux n'a pu rappeler les merveilleux talents de Fancioulle, ni s'élever jusqu'à la même *faveur*.

> (Since then, many mimes, rightfully appreciated in different countries, came to play before the court of ***; but none was able to recall the marvelous talents of Fancioulle, nor to attain the same *favor*.)

Now, the word *favor* is italicized in the text, although it is hard to see how favoritism and capital punishment could mix, or how one could lead to the other. Indeed, the concerns of execution and art would seem diametrically opposed, execution being designed to deprive the victim of a life that art might hope to render immortal. In a sense, though, Fancioulle gets exactly what he wants. His condemnation puts him pre-cisely where the artist wants to be: in the public eye. Here persecution and condemnation take on an entirely different resonance, making of the artist a martyr, elevating him to the role of saint and to the status of the divine, as foreshadowed during his performance.

> Ce bouffon allait, venait, riait, pleurait, se convulsait, avec une indestructible auréole autour de la tête, auréole invisible pour tous, mais visible pour moi, et où se mêlaient, dans un étrange amalgame, les rayons de l'Art et la gloire du Martyre. Fancioulle introduisait, par je ne sais quelle grâce spéciale, le divin et le surnaturel, jusque dans les plus extravagantes bouffonneries.

> (This clown came and went, laughed, cried, and grimaced, with an indestructible halo around his head, a halo invisible to all, but visible to me, and in which there mingled in a strange amalgam, the rays of Art and the glory of Martyrdom. Fancioulle displayed, by some inscrutable and special grace, the divine and the super-natural, even in his most outlandish antics.)

Fancioulle's performance reaches such heights that it will transcend the very death awaiting him; indeed, it reaches these heights *because* of the execution. The Prince, having enhanced the power of his adversary, unwittingly grants him the greatest favor imaginable: artistic immortality, achieved by a performance that will linger in the memory of the public and remain unmatched by his successors (Wing, 8).

The story of Fancioulle follows the standard trajectory of political repression, particularly in the case of censorship, and more particularly as it had been experienced by Baudelaire. The publicity that arose from the court case over *Les Fleurs du mal* gave the collection an immediate *succès de scandale*, and the judgment that was supposed to silence Baudelaire (*lui couper le sifflet*) served to accelerate the rise of his work to the highest favor. However, as in Fancioulle's case, the transcendence of the artistic product was to come at the expense of the artist himself; while Baudelaire did not lose his life over the legal battle, the resultant fines exacted a price he could ill afford.

Beyond the specific resonances with Baudelaire's own situation, there is inscribed within "Une mort héroïque" a more general commentary on the limitations of a power that wants to be absolute. The disappearance of Fancioulle delivers the Prince to his most redoubtable enemy: "Il ne connaissait d'ennemi dangereux que l'Ennui" (The only dangerous enemy he had was Boredom). Boredom, this "tyran du monde" (tyrant of the world) that beleaguers even the imperial life-style, reigns supreme when diversions are eliminated. The Prince's striking down of opposition corresponds to the basic practices of authority, those of resisting reform, of policing society and meaning, and of rendering symbolic systems, in Bakhtin's words, "monoaccentual" (Bakhtin and Volosinov, 44). The ideal goal of repression is, then, social "monoaccentuality"—or, in more practical terms; monotony. The Prince's regime thus tends inevitably toward the boredom he reviles. Paradoxically, if this monotony were ever fully achieved, it would eliminate the definition of power as repression; there would be nothing left to repress. The Prince finds himself in just such a situation and so, as it is hinted in the poem, he misses his "dear and inimitable Fancioulle." The master needs his slave, and the despot his victim.[22]

If Baudelaire succeeded in removing himself from the role of victim, it was not because he had shut up after *Les Fleurs du mal*—as if the

---

22. For another reading of "Une mort héroïque" as a strategy for disrupting power, see Wing, 5–12. See also Bachinger for a fascinating reading of one of Baudelaire's sources, Poe's "Hop Frog." Bachinger shows how Poe has similarly encoded another tale of tyranny, one dealing with Napoleon and George IV.

censors had managed to silence him. And yet it *appeared* as if they had: the prose poems caused very little stir. Baudelaire packaged his poetry carefully, with a keen sensitivity to bourgeois narcissism. Thus, an imperial reader, content that "Une mort héroïque" touched upon little more than the highly satisfactory outcome of an unsuccessful conspiracy (and the Orsini undertones, if noticed, would be even more satisfying), would look no further, and a more biting commentary could enter the text behind this mask of decorum.

The practice of masking was to become an important part of Baudelaire's esthetic code in the post-1857 period. In poems such as "Le Mauvais Vitrier" and "Une mort héroïque," the use of a narrative straw man to cover other activities had an incentive of considerable personal import: such texts were, in the letter of the law, illegal.[23] As a further deterrent, the laws also prohibited the publishing of any justification for acts qualified as criminal offenses,[24] a provision that would seem to apply to both "Le Mauvais Vitrier" and "Une mort héroïque." Furthermore, texts of a political nature were required to be deposited with the state prosecutor's office twenty-four hours before publication, with infractions leading to fines of up to five hundred francs (Duvergier, article 7 of 17 July 1849). In any case, a vaguely defined ordinance forbidding the crime of "inciting hatred or disdain of the government" served as a safety net to catch any undesirable texts otherwise eluding prosecution (Bellet, 14). Baudelaire's critiques were more biting and yet far more subtle than the famous political satires printed under the July Monarchy (see Terdiman, 149–97; Goldstein, chap. 4), and they were written under an even more repressive press regime; they thus needed to travel under cover, "*mis*cognito."

23. See note 3. That Baudelaire was not unversed in the intricacies of the arcane press laws of the Second Empire is demonstrated by his outrage when Billaut, the minister of the interior, forbade *Le Pays* to write about him: "*That is entirely illegal*; for I have not been convicted, only accused" (*Correspondance*, 1:418).

24. "[A]ny [published] defense of actions that are considered criminal by the penal code will be punished by imprisonment for a term of two to twenty-four months, and by a fine ranging from sixteen to one thousand francs"; Article 4, 27 July 1849 (Duvergier). Note that this statute was still in effect in 1857; the famous press decree of 17 February 1852 did not *replace* the earlier laws; it added to them. The principal changes effected by the press laws of the Second Empire consisted of taking press cases out of the hands of juries and attempting to squelch public discussion of these cases. For details on the intricacies of the press laws, see Pommier, Collins (118–35), and Bellet.

However, not all of Baudelaire's prose poems revolve around the court case, and the use of narrative masks extended beyond securing the poet's personal safety. Indeed, it was to become an integral part of a new esthetic program that began after Baudelaire's clash with the law. Although more pronounced by the time of the later prose poems, it was in evidence much earlier, perhaps first emblematized by a poem that would appear in the 1861 edition of the *Fleurs*, a piece appropriately entitled "Le Masque" (The mask). Here the poet portrays what he called an "allegorical statue," in which a face expressing horror and agony hides behind a mask of calm voluptuousness. In his *Salon de 1859* Baudelaire described his model (a statue by Ernest Christophe) in the following terms:

> The statue represents a naked woman of a fine and vigorous Florentine form . . . and which, seen from the front, offers the viewer a smiling and dainty countenance, a face worthy of the stage. . . . But by taking a step to the left or the right, you discover the secret of the allegory, the moral of the tale, I mean the real, contorted head, fainting from tears and agony. What had first enchanted your eyes was a mask. (*Oeuvres*, 2:678)

The statue is more, however, than an allegorical portrayal of the human condition; it can also be seen as a description of Baudelaire's own notion of allegory, predicated on incongruous dualisms (Hannoosh, 152–78), where the allegorical image is but a lie—one that Baudelaire's poetic vision undertakes to expose (see Hannoosh, 163). Yet Baudelaire's allegories do not impose themselves; rather, they remain resolutely ambiguous, indeterminable. It is thus entirely possible for a reader to interpret the text as "straight," to view, for example, "Une mort héroïque" as a consolidation of power instead of its subversion.

Just how one reads these allegories depends largely on one's ideological position, as well as how attached one is to this position. The artificiality of the bourgeois myths of progress, equality, and justice is not evident to those who, like the viewers of Christophe's statue, remain centered before them, and who have a vested interest in preserving the illusion. Baudelaire's allegorical, two-faced texts invite us to move off center, to take a step "to the left or the right" in order to see beyond the myths of order. Not everyone is susceptible to such an invitation: the imperturbable bourgeois of "Le Miroir" (The Mirror, 1864), who is transfixed by his own image without seeing his own repugnance, may never take the step. So the prose poems address themselves primarily to those whom these myths victimize and dispossess; they encourage the reader to look behind, for instance, the "mask" of the supernatural in "Le Mauvais Vitrier," or the benign allegory of political stability in "Une mort héroïque." The view they provide is decidedly off-center, offering glimpses of the tensions and inequities that commonplace language and proverbs strive to gloss over. By shifting the reader's perspective and making one see double, these poems make it difficult to maintain a single, coherent point of view (and consequently the untroubled smugness that such a view can lead to; see de Man, 166–86). This "binocularism" is what makes Baudelaire's later work infinitely more dangerous to the forces of order than the condemned poems of *Les Fleurs du mal*. When the imperial censors tried to clamp a lid on Baudelaire, they merely produced the pressure necessary for his language to ignite— "comme une explosion de gaz chez un vitrier."

Conclusion

In the introduction to this book I suggested that a crisis in representation, affecting not just the literary world but also the routine experience of much of the French population, prompted reactions that could be glimpsed in literary works of the revolutionary and postrevolutionary period. Organized as four general approaches—analogous to the four terms allowed by the opposition of the literal to the figurative—these reactions addressed the issue of semiotic disturbance.

By now the simplicity of this model must seem misleading. The texts at hand almost never raise questions of the adequacy or inadequacy of language explicitly; in addition, they seem engaged in maneuvers more subtle and complicated than a simple model should allow. Indeed, the complex entanglements of texts with particular historical circumstances means that discussions of representation have sometimes been obscured. Although it may at first appear paradoxical, these objections actually answer one another: it is *because* the works do not (indeed, *cannot*) address the problem of representation overtly that their reactions are perforce subtly *implied*; questions of representation are delicately entangled with other issues, ranging from politics to such cultural fads as Orientalism.

Reactions to the crisis in representation may never have been openly elaborated (nor, most often, consciously formulated) as an agenda in these works, but they do not necessarily lose their persuasive force as a result. To the contrary, their very invisibility conveys a sense of natural-ness, a "taken-for-granted-ness" that empowers them. Acts of fiction, as I argued at the beginning of this study, succeed by concealing aspects of their fictionality. As Baudelaire's poetry exemplifies so brilliantly, the pro-moting of misrecognition figures as an essential component of fiction, even when, as in "Le masque," this misrecognition itself is thematized.

Not surprisingly, it is Baudelaire who was, to my knowledge, the first to reflect on the way in which literature operates under contextual cover. The reflection occurs in his essay on the esthetics of Constantin Guys, "The Painter of Modern Life," where Baudelaire muses on the composite nature of the beautiful:

> The beautiful is composed of an eternal, invariable element, the quantity of which is excessively difficult to determine, and of a relative, circumstantial element, which could be, as you wish, alternately or all together, era, fashion, morality, passion. Without this second element, which is like the pleasing, titillating, appetiz-ing glaze of the divine cake, the first element would be indigest-ible, unappreciable, neither adapted nor appropriate for human nature. I defy anyone to find a single example of beauty that does not contain these two elements.... Even in the most frivolous work of a refined artist... this duality is to be found; *the eternal part of beauty will be simultaneously veiled and expressed*, if not by fashion, at least by the particular temperament of the author. (2:685; my emphasis)

Although Baudelaire's invocation of eternal or universal aspects of art may seem overstated for today's sensibilities, his assertion of the impor-tance of the ephemeral and the contemporary are unusually insightful. Reference to particularities, and the incorporation of subjects of local concern, anchored in time, is *necessary*, he suggests, for the most gen-eral aspects of a work to become meaningful. Moreover, this meaningful-ness can be expressed only in disguise, "veiled," as it were, by the very particularities that make it accessible.

It is their use of such local and contemporary elements that makes the texts of Sade, Balzac, Nerval, and Baudelaire especially rich examples of the dynamic of symbolic resolution. As Baudelaire suggests, the superim-position of the local upon more general concerns achieves two things.

First, it places abstract constructions like otherness or esthetics in terms that are familiar and intelligible for the contemporary reader. At the same time, however, the local, often anecdotal overlay *masks* the more abstract subtext, thereby promoting the misrecognition necessary for symbolic resolution to succeed. For example, Balzac's "realist" descriptions, which by their very seamlessness create a kind of nineteenth-century virtual reality, persuade the reader of the narrator's objectivity and of his anchoring in the "here and now." Yet as we saw in Chapter 3, the *real* effect of what Barthes called the Balzacian "effet de réel" is to grant Balzac the authority to deal with the "there and then." By investing his representation with the authority we usually reserve for reality, he manages to revise our notions of a past for which Balzac himself is nostalgic.

I would be inclined to expand Baudelaire's definition of esthetics to include a multitude of veils, encompassing a range of interconnected levels of generality. What impresses one in the texts we have examined here is the way in which these veils are enmeshed with one another. In *Philosophy in the Bedroom*, for example, we saw how a particular, lewd intrigue of sexual education was invested with symbolic power by drawing on other, more general concerns. Sade lends libertinism philosophic authority by grounding it in a thoroughly classical definition of nature, and the novel draws much of its affective power by riding on the coattails of local perceptions of corruption among the high aristocracy at the end of the ancien régime, that in turn played on the more generalized fear of the "indistinguishable Other." In Sade all of these tensions are aligned with the anxiety regarding *figures*, a term that takes on both graphic and linguistic forms, and that marks perversion of every sort. In Balzac, Nerval, and Baudelaire, the configurations are every bit as powerful. Although visible almost nowhere, concerns regarding figurality are present everywhere, informing Balzac's use of science and revolutionary history; Nerval's travels, translations, and dreams; and Baudelaire's subversion of commonplaces and common sense.

It is, I believe, this "many-layeredness" that makes these texts especially powerful. However, by multiple layers I do not mean the more or less generic "richness" we invoke when we suggest that a text can accommodate a number of different readings. Although as much can indeed be said of these texts (or, in fact, of any text), what has interested me here is principally the way in which multiple layers are interfolded within a given, single reading. Layering allows the crisis of representation—which can be thought of as one of the common denominators of the texts we have examined—to find significantly different expressions, differentiated not just by the various modes that inflect them (here, the modes of collusion, denial, reconstruction, and subversion), but also through more local or historically anchored themes, stories, and even details. In this light we see "local color" as more than incidental embellishment: the very toponymy of Parisian streets takes on considerable importance in Nerval's *Aurélia*, and nineteenth-century grooming figures as a revelatory emblem in a text like Balzac's *César Birotteau*.

If we can see how these texts operate—if we can recognize, that is, their misrecognitions—it is because our relationship to the text is different. What was local and familiar for various nineteenth-century readers is already estranged for us. We cannot be lulled into a sense of security by Balzac's descriptions, for instance, because these passages secure a social reality belonging to another age; similarly, when Baudelaire undermines commonsensical notions and commonplace language, he is meddling with a notion of banality that is no longer entirely ours.

This is not to say that the themes subtending the works of authors like Sade, Balzac, Nerval, and Baudelaire no longer concern us; rather, the ways in which they negotiate these issues no longer have the same effect. There is a sense in which fictions, if they are to maintain their force, require constant renegotiation; the terms linking text, context, and reader will always be reworked, new bricolages arising from the dismantled parts of the old. A volume could be written on the incarnations—both literary and otherwise—of any one of the themes we have reviewed. Thus the problem of the "indistinguishable Other," removed from debates about figurative language or the tradition of *libertinage*, resurfaces in other compelling configurations throughout our own century. The fear of just such a presence prompted Nazi attempts to catalogue characteristics (beginning with circumcision and extending to physiologies that rivaled Balzac's) that could be relied on as "symptoms" of Jewishness; when "natural" signs of difference were found wanting, the imposition of a conventional one— the yellow star—helped to achieve the desired recognizability. In the United States, fear of the unrecognizable Other came to center stage during the early years of the cold war; popular films like *The Invasion of the Body Snatchers* (1956), in which clones replaced their originals and infiltrated society, played off the McCarthy-inspired fears of omnipresent Communists. As the threats of the cold war retreated, the fiction again became available for appropriation and renegotiation, which this time has occurred in terms strangely resonant of Sade's "viral fiction": in the 1990s, the indistinguishable Other, the source of almost unchecked paranoia, has become the HIV-positive.

Cases such as these, where the line between public discourse and fiction has blurred, highlight the importance of careful contextual reading. In the end, the manipulation of signs becomes an issue of power, with very real social and political implications. As we have seen in an array of postrevolutionary texts, fictions overlay oppositions in ways that are often arbitrary, but that strive not to appear so. This arbitrariness can be seen in the disparate uses that single images have been made to serve. Just as revolutionary engravings employed the image of Hercules battling the Hydra (see Chapter 1) for radically incompatible purposes, so various authors (most notably Sade and Balzac) hijacked the notion of nature to serve vastly different ends. In these rhetorical struggles for power, each party faces the task of asserting the naturalness of its associations, as well as that of demonstrating the arbitrariness of others. Current public fictions continue to enact similar maneuvers. Thus in today's gender debates, for example, traditionalists may attempt to align such registers as anatomy, gender, and sexual orientation *in parallel* (suggesting, then, that one's orientation and behavior should *naturally* conform to one's anatomy); the tactic of opponents in this debate has consisted largely of asserting that these registers obey no natural or necessary parallelism.

If symbolic behavior in general, and writing in particular, can only enact its solutions symbolically, then this book can claim no special exemptions. Interpretations of symbolic acts are symbolic acts themselves, and they succeed only insofar as they mask their own strategies, or insofar as the reader shares their *partis pris*. Like many of the narratives examined in the preceding pages, interpretations tend to legitimate themselves by appealing to discourses of perceived legitimacy. Thus a critical work that rides on the coattails of cultural studies—or semiotics, feminism, deconstruction, or other "sanctioned" academic approaches—commands greater attention than one which appeals to mysticism or biography, both of which have been important principles of analysis at different times in the past. Yet if, in the end, interpretation consists of nothing more than a mediation between fictions, of using one bricolage to construct another, how can readings be anything but equally illegitimate?

This question, which threatens the authority of all discourses, is almost paralyzing. However, one's own participation in the very problematic one analyzes does not necessarily invalidate, a priori, one's conclusions. One need not be entirely divorced from the object of study in order to understand some of its workings, and one need not possess the last word in order to have something to say. Certainly we all grind axes (personal, disciplinary, social, political) to which we are more or less oblivious. For example, it is only very much in retrospect that I have reflected on my selection of authors for this volume—or, more to the point, on the authors I did not select. It occurs to me that the omission of women authors is significant for a variety of reasons, not the least of which is that for women authors of the period, the "trouble in representation" I have discussed is something of a *luxury*. It presupposes an initial *access* to representation, from which women were, to a large extent, both politically and culturally barred.

This kind of omission, while in some sense a *necessary* (if unmeditated) gesture before my discussion of representation could be opened, defines the limits and shortcomings of the enterprise. Nevertheless, while interpretation can never think its own unthought premises, one's own selective blindness does not bar one from detecting the blind spots of others. Analysis, then, both reveals and obscures; to borrow Baudelaire's words once again, we might say that interpretations will always be "simultaneously veiled and expressed." A study demonstrating this would not focus on texts like *La comédie humaine* or *Le Spleen de Paris*; rather, it would provide critical readings of earlier interpretations, amounting to something like a cultural history of Balzac or Baudelaire criticism.

But that, alas, would be another story.

Appendix

———————————————— • ————————————————

Le Mauvais Vitrier

Il y a des natures purement contemplatives et tout à fait impropres à l'action, qui cependant, sous une impulsion mystérieuse et inconnue, agissent quelquefois avec une rapidité dont elles se seraient crues elles-mêmes incapables.

Tel qui, craignant de trouver chez son concierge une nouvelle chagrinante, rôde lâchement devant sa porte sans oser rentrer, tel qui garde quinze jours une lettre sans la décacheter, ou ne se résigne qu'au bout de six mois à opérer une démarche nécessaire depuis un an, se sentent quelquefois brusquement précipités vers l'action par une force irrésistible, comme la flèche d'un arc. Le moraliste et le médecin, qui prétendent tout savoir, ne peuvent pas expliquer d'où vient si subitement une si folle énergie à ces âmes paresseuses et voluptueuses, et comment, incapables d'accomplir les choses les plus simples et les plus nécessaires, elles trouvent à une certaine minute un courage de luxe pour exécuter les actes les plus absurdes et même les plus dangereux.

Un de mes amis, le plus inoffensif rêveur qui ait existé, a mis une fois le feu à une forêt pour voir, disait-il, si le feu prenait avec autant de facilité qu'on l'affirme généralement. Dix fois de suite, l'expérience manqua; mais, à la onzième, elle réussit beaucoup trop bien.

Un autre allumera un cigare à côté d'un tonneau de poudre, *pour voir, pour savoir, pour tenter la destinée*, pour se contraindre lui-même à faire preuve d'énergie, pour faire le joueur, pour connaître les plaisirs de l'anxiété, pour rien, par caprice, par désoeuvrement.

C'est une espèce d'énergie qui jaillit de l'ennui et de la rêverie; et ceux en qui elle se manifeste si inopinément sont, en général, comme je l'ai dit, les plus indolents et les plus rêveurs des êtres.

Un autre, timide à ce point qu'il baisse les yeux même devant les regards des hommes, à ce point qu'il lui faut rassembler toute sa pauvre volonté pour entrer dans un café ou passer devant le bureau d'un théâtre, où les contrôleurs lui paraissent investis de la majesté de Minos, d'Eaque et de Rhadamante, sautera brusquement au cou d'un vieillard qui passe à côté de lui et l'embrassera avec enthousiasme devant la foule étonnée.

Pourquoi? Parce que . . . parce que cette physionomie lui était irrésist-iblement sympathique? Peut-être; mais il est plus légitime de supposer que lui-même il ne sait pas pourquoi.

J'ai été plus d'une fois victime de ces crises et de ces élans, qui nous autorisent à croire que des Démons malicieux se glissent en nous et nous font accomplir, à notre insu, leurs plus absurdes volontés.

Un matin je m'étais levé maussade, triste, fatigué d'oisiveté, et poussé, me semblait-il, à faire quelque chose de grand, une action d'éclat; et j'ouvris la fenêtre, hélas!

(Observez, je vous prie, que l'esprit de mystification qui chez quel-ques personnes, n'est pas le résultat d'un travail ou d'une combinaison, mais d'une inspiration fortuite, participe beaucoup, ne fût-ce que par l'ardeur du désir, de cette humeur, hystérique selon les médecins, sa-tanique selon ceux qui pensent un peu mieux que les médecins, qui nous pousse sans résistance vers une foule d'actions dangereuses ou inconvenantes.)

La première personne que j'aperçus dans la rue, ce fut un vitrier dont le cri perçant, discordant, monta jusqu'à moi à travers la lourde et sale atmosphère parisienne. Il me serait d'ailleurs impossible de dire pourquoi je fus pris à l'égard de ce pauvre homme d'une haine aussi soudaine que despotique.

«—Hé! hé!» et je lui criai de monter. Cependant je réfléchissais, non sans quelque gaieté, que, la chambre étant au sixième étage et l'escalier fort étroit, l'homme devait éprouver quelque peine à opérer son ascen-sion et accrocher en maint endroit les angles de sa fragile marchandise.

Enfin il parut: j'examinai curieusement toutes ses vitres, et je lui dis: «Comment? vous n'avez pas de verres de couleur? des verres roses, rouges, bleus, des vitres magiques, des vitres de paradis? Impudent que vous êtes! vous osez vous promener dans des quartiers pauvres, et vous n'avez pas même de vitres qui fassent voir la vie en beau!» Et je le poussai vivement vers l'escalier, où il trébucha en grognant.

Je m'approchai du balcon et je me saisis d'un petit pot de fleurs, et quand l'homme reparut au débouché de la porte, je laissai tomber per-pendiculairement mon engin de guerre sur le rebord postérieur de ses crochets; et le choc le renversant, il acheva de briser sous son dos toute sa pauvre fortune ambulatoire qui rendit le bruit éclatant d'un palais de cristal crevé par la foudre.

Et, ivre de ma folie, je lui criai furieusement: «La vie en beau! la vie en beau!»

Ces plaisanteries nerveuses ne sont pas sans péril, et on peut souvent les payer cher. Mais qu'importe l'éternité de la damnation à qui a trouvé dans une seconde l'infini de la jouissance?

The Bad Glazier

There are people of a purely contemplative nature, wholly unsuited to action, who nevertheless, under a mysterious and unknown impulse, sometimes act with a speed of which they would have believed themselves incapable.

Such as he who, fearing his concierge has some distressing news for him, loiters in front of his door for an hour without daring to enter; or he who holds onto a letter for a fortnight without opening it, or who finally resigns himself after six months to take some action that has been pressing for a year; sometimes they feel suddenly thrown headlong into action by an irresistible force, like an arrow from a bow. The moralist and the physician, who claim to know everything, cannot explain whence comes so suddenly such a mad energy to these lazy and voluptuous souls, and how, unable to accomplish the simplest and most necessary of things, they find at a given moment a wealth of initiative to perform the most absurd and often the most dangerous acts.

A friend of mine, the most harmless dreamer there ever was, once set fire to a forest in order to see, so he maintained, whether fire caught as easily as people say. Ten times in a row the experiment failed; but, on the eleventh try it worked all too well.

Another might light up a cigar next to a powder keg, *to see, to find out, to tempt fate*, to make a show of strength, to play the gambler, to experience the pleasures of anxiety, for no reason, because of a whim, out of boredom.

It is a kind of energy that springs from boredom and reverie; and those in whom it manifests itself so markedly are, in general, as I have said, the most languid and dreamy of beings.

Another fellow—so shy that he drops his gaze when people look at him, that it takes all the willpower he can muster just to enter a café or walk past the box office of a theater, where the ushers seem to him to be invested with all the majesty of Minos, Aeacus, and Rhadamanthus—will suddenly leap at the neck of an old man passing by and kiss him fervently in front of the astonished crowd.

Why? Because... because he found that particular face unbearably attractive? Perhaps; but it is closer to the truth to assume that he himself does not know why.

On more than one occasion I have been victim to these attacks and impulses, which authorize us to believe that malicious demons slip into us and make us act out unwittingly their most absurd wishes.

One morning I woke up gloomy, sad, tired of being idle, and moved, so it seemed to me, to do something grand, to make a commotion; and I opened the window, alas!

(Please note that the talent for practical jokes which, among some, is not the result of calculation or scheming, but of lucky inspiration, partakes greatly, be it only by the strength of desire, of that humor, called hysterical by doctors, satanic by those who think a bit better than doctors, that drives us effortlessly toward a whole host of dangerous or inappropriate actions.)

The first person I saw in the road was a glazier whose tuneless, strident call rose all the way up to me through the heavy, dirty air of Paris. It would be impossible for me to say why I felt for this poor fellow a hatred as sudden as it was despotic.

"Hey, you!" and I called for him to come up. Meanwhile I reflected, with no small measure of glee, that, the room being on the sixth floor, and the stairway quite narrow, the fellow would experience some difficulty in making his ascent, and would catch the corners of his fragile merchandise at every turn.

Finally he appeared. I browsed through his panes, and then said, "What? You have no colored glass? No pink glass, nor red, nor blue? No magic panes, panes of paradise? How could you be so impudent! You dare to walk through poor neighborhoods, and you don't even carry the panes that might make life beautiful!" And I pushed him roughly toward the stairs, where he stumbled with a groan.

I approached the balcony and picked up a small pot of flowers, and when the fellow reappeared from the doorway below, I dropped my war machine perpendicularly upon the back edge of his peddler's pack; the shock knocked him over, and he thoroughly shattered under his back his entire poor, ambulatory fortune, which made the resounding noise of a crystal palace struck by lightning.

And drunk with my madness, I shrieked at him: "Make life beautiful! Make life beautiful!"

These spirited jokes are not without danger, and one often pays dearly for them. But what does an eternity of damnation matter to one who has found in a second the boundlessness of pleasure?

Works Cited

Althusser, Louis. "Ideology and Ideological State Apparatuses." In *Lenin and Philosophy and Other Essays,* Translated by Ben Brewster, 131–41. London: NLB, 1971.

Amossy, Ruth, and Elisheva Rosen. *Les Discours du cliché.* Paris: CDU et SEDES réunis, 1982.

Avni, Ora. *The Resistance of Reference.* Baltimore: Johns Hopkins University Press, 1990.

Bachinger, Katrina. "Together (or Not Together) against Tyranny: Poe, Byron, and Napoleon Upside Down in 'Hop-Frog.'" *Texas Studies in Literature and Language* 33; no. 3 (Fall 1991): 373–402.

Bakhtin, M. M., and Volosinov, V. N. *Le Marxisme et la philosophie du langage.* Paris: Editions de Minuit, 1977.

Balzac, Honoré de. *La Comédie humaine.* 12 vols. Paris: Gallimard, 1976–81.

———. *Oeuvres diverses.* 3 vols. Edited by Henri Longon. Paris: Conard, 1940.

Barbéris, Pierre. *Balzac et le mal du siècle.* Paris: Gallimard, 1970.

Barthes, Roland. *Sade, Fourier, Loyola.* Translated by Richard Miller. New York: Hill and Wang, 1976.

———. *S/Z.* Paris: Seuil, 1970. 1st American ed., translated by Richard Miller. New York: Hill and Wang, 1974.

Baudelaire, Charles. *Correspondance.* 2 vols. Paris: Gallimard, 1973.

———. *Oeuvres complètes.* 2 vols. Paris: Gallimard, 1975.

Bellet, Roger. *Presse et journalisme sous le Second Empire.* Paris: Armand Colin, 1967.

Benjamin, Walter. *Charles Baudelaire: A Lyric Poet in the Era of High Capitalism.* Translated by H. Zohn. London: NLB, 1973.

Bennington, Geoff. "Sade: Laying Down the Law." *Oxford Literary Review* 6, no. 2 (1984): 38–56.

Bertaud, Jean-Paul. *La Vie quotidienne en France au temps de la Révolution.* Paris: Hachette, 1983.

Bierman, John. *Napoleon III and his Carnival Empire.* New York: St. Martin's Press, 1988.

Blanche, Sylvestre. *De l'état actuel du traitement de la folie en France.* Paris: A. Gardembas, 1840.

Boime, Albert. *Hollow Icons: The Politics of Sculpture in Nineteenth-Century France.* Kent: Kent State University Press, 1987.

Bonnefin, Aimé. *Sacre des rois de France.* Limoges: Touron et fils, 1982.

Bougainville, Louis-Antoine, baron de. *Voyage autour du monde par la frégate du roi "la Boudeuse" et la flûte "l'Etoile," en 1766, 1767, 1768, 1769.* Paris: 1770.

Bowman, Frank Paul. "Du romantisme au positivisme: Alfred Maury." *Romantisme* 21–22 (1978): 35–44.

———. *French Romanticism: Intertextual and Interdisciplinary Readings.* Baltimore: Johns Hopkins University Press, 1990.

Brooks, Peter. "Narrative Transaction and Transference (Unburying *Le Colonel Chabert*)." *Novel: A Forum on Fiction* 15 (1982): 101–10.

Brunier, Christian. "Tchécoslovaquie 1968." In *Résistances civiles*, 77–83. Montargis, France: Non-Violence Actualité, 1983.

Byrne, P. W. "The Moral of *Les Liaisons dangereuses.*" *Essays in French Literature* 23 (November 1986): 1–18.

Brunot, Ferdinand. *Histoire de la langue française.* 13 vols. Paris: Colin, 1905–1969.

Buffon, Georges-Louis. *Oeuvres complètes* Vol. I. Paris: Société des publications illustrées, 1851.

Burton, Richard. *Baudelaire in 1859: A Study in the Sources of Poetic Creativity.* Cambridge: Cambridge University Press, 1988.

Certeau, Michel de, Dominique Julia, and Jacques Revel. *Une Politique de la langue. La Révolution française et les patois: l'enquête de Grégoire.* Paris: Gallimard, 1975.

Chambers, Ross. "The Parasite as Hero." Presented at the Sixteenth Annual Nineteenth-Century French Studies Colloquium, Norman, Oklahoma, October 1990.

———. "Récits d'aliénés, récits aliénés: Nerval et John Percival." *Poétique* 53 (1953): 72–90.

———. *Room for Maneuver: Reading (the) Oppositional (in) Literature.* Chicago: University of Chicago Press, 1991.

———. *Story and Situation: Narrative Seduction and the Power of Fiction.* Minneapolis: University of Minnesota Press, 1984.

Chateaubriand, François-René. *René.* In vol. 1 of *Oeuvres romanesques et voyages.* Edited by Maurice Regard. Paris: Gallimard, 1969.

———. *Itinéraire de Paris à Jérusalem.* In vol. 5 of *Oeuvres de Chateaubriand.* Paris: Garnier, 1859.

Cheveux naturels, vieille perruque, et faux toupet: Chronique cochinchinoise de 1830 à 1850. Paris: Imprimerie centrale de Napoléon Chaiz, 1850.

Chomsky, Noam. *Cartesian Linguistics: A Chapter in the History of Rationalist Thought,* New York: Harper and Row, 1966.

Clifford, James. "On Collecting Art and Culture." In *The Cultural Studies Reader*, edited by Simon During, 49–73. New York: Routledge, 1993.

Collins, Irene. *The Government and the Newspaper Press in France, 1814–1881.* Oxford: Oxford University Press, 1959.

Conisbee, Philip. *Painting in Eighteenth-Century France.* Ithaca: Cornell University Press, 1981.

Constant, Benjamin. *Adolphe: Anecdote trouvée dans les papiers d'un inconnu.* Edited by C. P. Courtney. New York: Blackwell, 1989.

Cuvier, Georges. *Discours sur les révolutions de la surface du globe.* Paris: 1822. Translated as *Essay on the Theory of the Earth.* Translated by Robert Kerr. Edinburgh: Blackwood, 1830.

Darmon, Pierre. *Trial by Impotence: Virility and Marriage in Pre-Revolutionary France.* Translated by Paul Keegan. London: Hogarth, 1985.

Darnton, Robert. *The Great Cat Massacre.* New York: Basic Books, 1984.

Davidson, Donald. "What Metaphors Mean." In *Inquiries into Truth and Interpretation,* 245–64. Oxford: Oxford University Press, 1984.

Dayan, Peter. *Nerval et ses pères: Portrait en trois volets, deux gonds, et un cadenas.* Genèva: Droz, 1992.

DeJean, Joan. *Literary Fortifications: Rousseau, Laclos, Sade.* Princeton: Princeton University Press, 1984

De Man, Paul. *Allegories of Reading.* New Haven: Yale University Press, 1979.
———. *Blindness and Insight.* Minneapolis: University of Minnesota Press, 1983.
———. "The Epistemology of Metaphor." *Critical Inquiry,* 5 (Autumn, 1978), 13–30.

Derrida, Jacques. "Cogito et histoire de la folie." In *L'Ecriture et la différence,* 51–97. Paris: Seuil, 1967.
———. *De la grammatologie.* Paris: Editions de Minuit, 1967.
———. "La différance." In *Théorie d'ensemble.* Edited by Philippe Sollers, 43–68. Paris: Seuil, 1968.
———. *L'Ecriture et la différence.* Paris, Seuil, 1967.
———. "White Mythology: Metaphor in the Text of Philosophy." In *Margins of Philosophy.* Translated by Alan Bass, 207–72. Chicago: University of Chicago Press, 1982.

Diderot, Denis. *Oeuvres.* Edited by André Billy. Paris, Gallimard, 1951.

Diderot, Denis, and Jean d'Alembert, eds. *Encyclopédie, ou Dictionnaire raisonné des sciences, des arts et des métiers, par une société de gens de lettres.* 17 vols. Paris, 1751–72.

Douthwaite, Julia. *Exotic Women: Literary Heroines and Cultural Strategies in Ancien Régime France.* Philadelphia: University of Pennsylvania Press, 1992.

Dumarsais, César. *Traité des tropes.* Paris: 1729, reprinted as *Les Tropes,* by César Dumarsais and Pierre Fontanier. Geneva: Slatkine, 1967 [1818].

Duvergier, J. B. *Collection complète des lois, décrets, ordonnances, règlements et avis du conseil d'état.* Paris: Editions officielles, annual.

Eco, Umberto. *Interpretation and Overinterpretation.* Cambridge: Cambridge University Press, 1992.

Esquirol, Jean-Etienne-Dominique. *Des Maladies mentales considérées sous les rapports médical, hygiénique, et médico-légal.* Paris: Baillière, 1838.
———. "Manie." *Dictionnaire des sciences médicales.* Vol. 30. Paris: Panckouke, 1812–1822.

Felman, Shoshana. *La Folie et la chose littéraire.* Paris: Seuil, 1978.

Flaubert, Gustave. *Oeuvres complètes.* 2 vols. Paris: Seuil, 1964.

Foucault, Michel. *Histoire de la folie à l'âge classique.* Paris: Gallimard, 1972.
———. *Les Mots et les choses.* Paris: Gallimard, 1966.

————, ed. *Herculine Barbin dite Alexina B.* Paris: Gallimard, 1978.

Foville, Achille. "Délire." In vol. 11 of *Nouveau Dictionnaire de médecine.* Edited by Dr. Jaccoud. Paris: Baillière et fils, 1872.

————. "Folie." In vol. 15 of *Nouveau Dictionnaire de médecine.* Edited by Dr. Jaccoud. Paris: Baillière et Fils, 1872.

Fromentin, Eugène. *Dominique.* In *Oeuvres complètes.* Edited by Guy Sagnes, 367–564. Paris: Gallimard, 1984.

Friedman, Geraldine. "Baudelaire's Theory of Practice: Ideology and Difference in 'Les yeux des pauvres.' " *PMLA* 104, no. 3 (May 1989): 317–28.

Friguglietti, James. "Gilbert Romme and the Making of the French Republican Calendar." In *The French Revolution in Culture and Society,* edited by David Troyansky, Alfred Cismaru and Norwood Andrew, Jr., 13–22. New York: Greenwood, 1991.

Gaillard, Françoise. "Aurélia ou la question du nom." In *Le Rêve et la vie.* 237–47. Paris: C.D.U. et SEDES réunis, 1986.

————. "Désordre social et ordre romanesque: une lecture de *La théorie de la démarche.*" *Nineteenth-Century French Studies* 21, nos. 3 and 4 (1993): 277–91.

Geertz, Clifford. *The Interpretation of Cultures.* New York: Basic Books, 1973.

Girard, René. *Violence and the Sacred.* Translated by Patrick Gregory. Baltimore: Johns Hopkins University Press: 1977.

Goldstein, Robert. *Censorship of Political Caricature in Nineteenth-Century France.* Kent: Kent State University Press, 1989.

Gordon, Rae Beth. *Ornament, Fantasy, and Desire in Nineteenth-Century French Literature.* Princeton: Princeton University Press, 1992.

Graffigny, Françoise d'Issembourg et d'Happoncourt de. *Lettres d'une péruvienne.* Paris: Flammarion, 1983.

Greenblatt, Stephen. *Marvelous Possessions: The Wonder of the New World.* Chicago: University of Chicago Press, 1991.

————. "Toward a Poetics of Culture." In *The New Historicism.* H. Aram Veeser, ed. New York: Routledge, 1989.

Greimas, A. J. and F. Rastier. "The Interaction of Semiotic Constraints." *Yale French Studies* 41 (1968): 86–105.

Hampson, Norman. *The Enlightenment.* London: Penguin, 1968.

Hannoosh, Michele. *Baudelaire and Caricature: From the Comic to an Art of Modernity.* University Park: Pennsylvania State University Press, 1992.

Harari, Josué. "D'Une Raison à l'autre." *Studies on Voltaire and the Eighteenth Century* 230. Oxford: Voltaire Foundation, (1985): 273–82.

————. *Scenarios of the Imaginary: Theorizing the French Enlightenment.* Ithaca: Cornell University Press, 1987.

Harrap's Slang Dictionary. Bromley: Harrap Books, 1983.

Heck, Francis. " 'Le Mauvais Vitrier': A Literary Transfiguration." *Nineteenth Century French Studies* 14 (Fall–Winter 1985–86): 260–68.

Huffer, Lynne. "*Aurélia,* une intimité illusoire." *Iris* 11, no. 2 (1986): 39–50.

Hugo, Victor. *Oeuvres complètes.* 18 vols. Paris: Vve. Alexandre Houssaix, 1869.

Hunt, Lynn. *The Family Romance of the French Revolution.* Berkeley and Los Angeles: University of California Press, 1992.

————. "The Many Bodies of Marie Antoinette: Political Pornography and the Problem of the Feminine in the French Revolution." In *Eroticism and the Body Politic*, 108–130. Baltimore: Johns Hopkins University Press, 1991.

————. *Politics, Culture, and Class in the French Revolution*. Berkeley and Los Angeles: University of California Press, 1984.

————, ed. *Eroticism and the Body Politic*. Baltimore: Johns Hopkins University Press, 1991.

Ido, Keiko. "Les Expressions de la perversité chez Baudelaire: La Méthode d'Edgar Poe et la genèse du "Mauvais Vitrier." *Etudes de Langue et de Littérature Françaises* 46 (March 1985): 52–67.

Jakobson, Roman. "Two Aspects of Language and Two Types of Aphasic Disturbances." In *Studies on Child Language and Aphasia*, 49–74. The Hague: Mouton, 1971.

Jameson, Fredric. *The Political Unconscious*. Ithaca: Cornell University Press, 1981.

Jeanneret, Michel. "La Folie est un rêve: Nerval et le docteur Moreau de Tours." *Romantisme* (1980): 59–75.

————. *La lettre perdue: écriture et folie dans l'oeuvre de Nerval*. Paris: Flammarion, 1978.

————. "Sur le *Voyage en Orient* de Nerval." *Cahiers Roumains d'Etudes Littéraires* 4 (1980): 29–46.

Johnson, Barbara. *The Critical Difference*. Baltimore: Johns Hopkins University Press, 1980.

————. *Défigurations du langage poétique*. Paris: Seuil, 1979.

Johnson, Dorothy. "Corporality and Communication: The Gestural Revolution of Diderot, David, and *The Oath of the Horatii*." *Art Bulletin* 71 (March 1989): 92–113.

Kaplan, Ed. *Baudelaire's Prose Poems: The Esthetic, the Ethical, and the Religious in the Parisian Prowler*. Athens: University of Georgia Press, 1990.

Kennedy, Emmet. *A Cultural History of the French Revolution*. New Haven: Yale University Press, 1989.

Krauss, Rosalind E. *The Optical Unconscious*. Cambridge: MIT Press, 1993.

Kristeva, Julia. *La Révolution du langage poétique: l'avant-garde à la fin du 19e siècle: Lautréamont et Mallarmé*. Paris: Seuil, 1976.

Kselman, Thomas. *Death and the Afterlife in Modern France*. Princeton: Princeton University Press, 1993.

Laborde, A. M. *Sade romancier*. Neuchâtel: Editions de la Baconnière, 1974.

Lacan, Jacques. *Ecrits*. Vol. 2. Paris: Seuil, 1966.

LaCapra, Dominick. *Madame Bovary on Trial*. Ithaca: Cornell University Press, 1982.

Laclos, Pierre Ambroise François Choderlos de. *Les Liaisons dangereuses*. Paris: Flammarion, 1981.

Lamartine, Alphonse de. *Oeuvres poétiques complètes*. Paris: Gallimard, 1991.

Landes, Joan. *Women and the Public Sphere in the Age of the French Revolution*. Ithaca: Cornell University Press, 1988.

Le Brun, Annie. *Sade—A Sudden Abyss*. Translated by Camille Naish. San Francisco: City Light Books, 1991.

Leuret, François. *Des indications à suivre dans le traitement moral de la folie.* Paris: Le Normant, 1846.

Lever, Maurice. *Donatien Alphonse François, marquis de Sade.* Paris: Fayard, 1991.

Lévi-Strauss, Claude. *La Pensée sauvage.* Paris: Plon, 1962.

———. *Tristes tropiques.* Paris: Plon, 1955.

Lotman, Y. M. "Le Mot et la langue dans la culture du siècle des Lumières." *Actes du Septième congrès international des Lumières, 1989,* in *Studies on Voltaire and the Eighteenth Century* 265. Oxford: Voltaire Foundation, (1989): 1567–74.

Marc, Charles. *De la folie considérée dans ses rapports avec les question médico-judiciaires.* Paris: J. B. Baillière, 1840.

Marini, Marcelle. "Chabert mort ou vif." *Littérature* 13 (1974): 92–112.

Marivaux, Pierre Carlet de Chamblain de. "Le Jeu de l'amour et du hasard." In *Thèâtre complet,* 274–92. Paris: Seuil, 1964.

Matthey, André. *Nouvelles recherches sur les maladies de l'esprit.* Paris: J. J. Paschoud, 1816.

Maury, Alfred. "Nouvelles observations sur les analogies des phénomènes du rêve et de l'aliénation mentale." In *Annales Médico-psychologiques,* 404–21. Paris: Masson, 1853.

Maza, Sarah. "The Diamond Necklace Affair Revisited (1785–1786): The Case of the Missing Queen." In *Eroticism and the Body Politic,* ed. Lynn Hunt, 108–30. Baltimore: Johns Hopkins University Press, 1991.

Montesquieu, Charles-Louis de. *Lettres Persanes.* Paris: Garnier-Flammarion, 1964.

Moreau de Tours, Jacques-Joseph. *Du Hachisch et de l'aliénation mentale.* Paris: Fortin, Masson, 1845.

Murphy, Steve. " 'Le Mauvais Vitrier' ou la crise du verre." *Romanic Review* 82, no. 3 (1990): 339–49.

Musset, Alfred de. *La Confession d'un enfant du siècle.* Paris: Gallimard [Folio], 1973.

Nerval, Gérard de. *Oeuvres.* 3 vols. Edited by Albert Béguin and Jean Richer. Paris: Gallimard, 1974.

———. *Oeuvres complètes.* 3 vols. Edited by Claude Pichois. Paris: Gallimard, 1984.

———. Preface to *Faust.* by Johann Wolfgang von Goethe. Translated by Gérard de Nerval. Paris: Garnier, [1828].

Ozouf, Mona. *La Fête révolutionnaire, 1789–1799.* Paris: Gallimard, 1976.

Pasco, Alan. *Balzacian Montage: Configuring La Comédie humaine.* Toronto: University of Toronto Press, 1991.

Petrey, Sandy. *Realism and Revolution: Balzac, Stendhal, Zola, and the Performances of History.* Ithaca: Cornell University Press, 1988.

Pizzorusso, Arnaldo. " 'Le Mauvais Vitrier,' ou l'impulsion inconnue." *Etudes Baudelairiennes VIII.* Neuchâtel: Editions de la Baconnière, 1976.

Pommier, Jean. *Autour de l'édition originale des Fleurs du mal.* Geneva: Slatkine, 1963.

Prendergast, Christopher. *The Order of Mimesis.* Cambridge: Cambridge University Press, 1986.

Pugh, Anthony. "The Ambiguity of *César Birotteau*." *Nineteenth-Century French Studies* 8, nos. 3–4 (1980): 173–89.

Renan, Ernest. "De l'origine du language." Part 2, *La Liberté de Penser*, no. 2 (1848): 64–83.

Rétif de la Bretonne, Nicolas Anne Edme. *Oeuvres érotiques*. Paris: Fayard, 1985.

Ribeiro, Aileen. *Fashion in the French Revolution*. New York: Holmes and Meier, 1988.

Richer, Jean. *Gérard de Nerval et les doctrines ésotériques*. Paris: Editions du Griffon d'Or, 1947.

Robiquet, Jean. *La Vie quotidienne au temps de la Révolution*. Paris: Hachette, 1938.

Rorty, Richard. *Contingency, Irony, and Solidarity*. Cambridge: Cambridge University Press, 1989.

Rosenblum, R. "A Source for David's *Horatii*." *Burlington Magazine* 112 (1970): 269–73.

Rousseau, Jean-Jacques. *Essai sur l'origine des langues*, Edited by Charles Porset. Bordeaux: Guy Ducros, 1969

———. *Oeuvres complètes*. Edited by Bernard Gagnebin and Marcel Raymond. 4 vols. Paris: Gallimard, 1959.

Sade, Donatien-Alphonse-François de. *Oeuvres complètes du Marquis de Sade*. Edited by Annie Le Brun. 15 vols. Paris: Société Nouvelle des Editions Pauvert, 1987.

Salin, Edouard. *La Civilisation mérovingienne*. Paris: Editions A. and J. Picard, 1987. (Originally published 1949)

Schama, Simon. *Citizens: A Chronicle of the French Revolution*. New York: Vintage, 1989.

Schofer, Peter. "Baudelaire's Theater of Social Cruelty." In *Theater and Society in French Literature*. French Literature Series 15. Columbia: University of South Carolina Press, (1988): 50–57.

Seylaz, J.-L. "Les Mots et la chose: Sur l'emploi des mots "amour" et "aimer" chez Mme de Merteuil et Valmont." *Revue d'Histoire Littéraire de la France* 82, no. 4 (1982): 559–74.

Sheriff, Mary. "Fragonard's Erotic Mothers and the Politics of Reproduction." In *Eroticism and the Body Politic*, edited by Lynn Hunt, Baltimore: Johns Hopkins University Press, 1991.

Sivert, Eileen. "Who's Who: Non-Characters in *Le Colonel Chabert*." *French Forum* 13, no. 2 (May 1988): 217–29.

Starobinski, Jean. *Portrait de l'artiste en saltimbanque*. Geneva: Skira, 1970.

———. *La Transparence et l'obstacle*. Paris: Gallimard, 1976.

Stewart, Philip, and Madeleine Therrien. "Aspects de texture verbale dans *Les liaisons dangereuses*." *Revue d'Histoire Littéraire de la France* 82, no. 4 (1982): 547–58.

Swiggers, P. "Catégories de langue et catégories de grammaire dans la théorie linguistique des Encyclopédistes." *Studies on Voltaire and the Eighteenth Century* 241. Oxford: Voltaire Foundation, (1986): 339–64.

Szasz, Thomas. *The Myth of Mental Illness*. New York: Hoeber-Harper, 1961.

Tardieu, Ambroise. *Etude médico-légale sur la folie*. Paris: J. B. Baillière et fils, 1872.

Terdiman, Richard. *Discourse/Counter-Discourse: The Theory and Practice of Symbolic Resistance in Nineteenth-Century France*. Ithaca: Cornell University Press, 1985.

Thompson, J. M. *Louis Napoleon and the Second Empire*. New York: Norton, 1967.

Todorov, Tzvetan. *Introduction à la littérature fantastique*. Paris: Seuil, 1970.

Torgovnick, Marianna. *Closure in the Novel*. Princeton: Princeton University Press, 1981.

Toumayan, Alain. *La Littérature et la hantise du Mal*. Lexington, Ky.: French Forum, 1987.

Voltaire. "Langues." *Dictionnaire philosophique*, in *Oeuvres complètes*. Paris: Garnier Frères, 1879.

———. *Oeuvres complètes de Voltaire*. Oxford: Voltaire Foundation, 1980.

Wing, Nathaniel. "Poets, Mimes, and Counterfeit Coins." *Paragraph: A Journal of Modern Critical Theory* 13, no. 1 (March 1990): 1–18.

Zola, Emile. *Le Ventre de Paris*. Paris: Garnier-Flammarion, 1971.

Index

DATE DUE

HIGHSMITH #45115